Cameron Wyllie spent his entire career in the teaching profession, first at Daniel Stewart's and Melville College, then at George Heriot's, both in Edinburgh. He is a regular contributor to the *Scotsman* on educational matters and has also written for the *Scotland on Sunday*, *Holyrood* magazine and *The Times*. He lives in Joppa, Edinburgh.

'An enlightening and honest look at what it's really like to educate and prepare young people for their future. Packed full of hysterical anecdotes, colourful characters and told with such a lightness of touch – this is an earnest, laugh-out loud memoir' EMUN ELLIOTT (actor)

'Cameron Wyllie's prose, like his teaching, is funny, warm, surprising and not quite like that offered by anyone else . . . one discovers Wyllie's most interesting virtue: his unerring eye for the truth' DAVID GREIG (playwright)

'A scrumptious selection box of a schoolteacher's anecdotes, musings and erudite observations . . . his book has a warm heart, a dry wit and a resilient aftertaste. It touches on a universal and everlasting truth: that education is not really about subjects and exams after all . . . A delight' JANEY JONES (novelist and children's author)

Is There a Pigeon in the Room?

My Life in Schools

Cameron Wyllie

BIRLINN

First published in 2022 by
Birlinn Ltd
West Newington House
10 Newington Road
Edinburgh
EH9 1QS

www.birlinn.co.uk

ISBN 978 1 78027 773 8

British Library Cataloguing in Publication Data
A catalogue record for this book is available from the British Library.

Typeset by Initial Typesetting Services, Edinburgh

Printed and bound by Clays Ltd, Elcograf S.p.A.

To everyone I have ever taught,
and particularly to Kevin

Contents

'And gladly would he learn and gladly teach'
Chaucer, *The Canterbury Tales*

The Silk Not Taken

My parents did not want me to be a teacher. They had both left school when they were fifteen, and although my father did well in his work, he always wanted his sons to make more money than he had. My mother, who had been very poor and very aware of it when she was the fractured, unhappy, pretty girl she was when she met my dad, hoarded money all her life – when she died there was £1,000 in each of five old handbags hidden in different parts of the house that my father did not know about: she was always ready to flee with cash in hand. So she too did not like the idea of my teaching.

My brother Jimmy, four years older, very tall, very handsome, very clever, had been dux of George Heriot's School, and had gone to Cambridge to study Law. As I was deciding what to do at university, he, at twenty-two, had done the hard bit of training necessary to qualify as a solicitor, after all the philosophy and punting and balls, and had set himself up with a job in London. So when I was filling out my own UCCA form, selecting the six choices was easy – five applications for Law in Scotland and one to study English at Edinburgh, this last only because the school demanded the 'safety net' application for something easier to get into. And that was that. Because I talked a lot and debated at school, my mother decided I would 'take silk' and be an advocate. She loved that phrase – 'take silk' – I was never entirely sure what it meant, and I doubt if she was. But silk was luxury, and we were a family who wore nylon shirts and plastic shoes, not because of vegetarian principles but because they were cheap. One day, in a court somewhere, she would watch me and I would be wearing silk.

My parents did not sin. My mother stopped smoking and my father stopped drinking on the same day in December 1963. I was six and it was ghastly. For years, every morning my mother had rolled herself ten astonishingly thin cigarettes in a Rizla machine and smoked them at regular intervals through the long days of housework and what for her

3

approximated to child-raising. I don't remember my father drinking, though he talked about drink a lot, for he was the third generation of his family to work in the whisky industry. He saw, he said, too many men turned into alcoholics by the ready availability of cheap, or free, booze. So he stopped when she stopped. It was not a good Christmas.

From then on their one regular concession to pleasurable living (apart from TV and sweeties) was having lunch out on a Saturday, followed by a film. In my later teenage years, I would go for lunch, but skip the cinema, since the choosing of the 'picture' was scarcely democratic – my mother had all the votes and liked slasher films and, more surprisingly, weepies. We would eat in cheap places with good service, which meant water and bread on the table and the menu being presented within thirty seconds of your arrival, preferably by an older waitress to whom my mother could talk and whom my father could tip generously. The food itself didn't matter in the slightest.

So one hot and sunny Saturday, walking to a pub for a lunch, the best bit of which would be the lime and soda which would accompany steak pie or scampi and chips, I said that I had decided I didn't want to study Law, that I wanted to pick up my English offer and I wanted to teach. My mother's disapproval was instantaneous – no silk, no one to defend her free of charge when her crimes were at last revealed (for Jimmy, my brother, was after all an 'English lawyer'). She said nothing, but simply allowed my father to say, as he was always going to, that if that's what I wanted, that's what I wanted. And it was.

*

There are many reasons why people become teachers, including the long holidays, the great pension and sometimes because they didn't become what they wanted to become in the first place. I was lucky that it was what I really wanted to do because teaching in a secondary school requires two things – you need to like young people, and you need to be interested in telling them about your subject; if you have these two things then teaching is the best possible job you could have. Though I was by no means an academic student, I enjoyed English at school and at university. And though I had many friends, I think, in the school staffroom – easier at the start of my career than at the end – generally I was always happier in the playground talking to kids. My working life passed so quickly, each year like a huge steadily revolving stone wheel, marked by events – plays, concerts, sports days, Leavers Balls, Founders Days, church services, exam diets, that were each year never quite the same. The doctor who did my medical on my entrance to the profession said I was chronically underweight; I started teaching wearing size 26 trousers. How did I get fatter, as indeed I did? Why is my hair no longer on my head but in my ears? And where are all these children now?

I loved university, but I'm not sure how much I learned. I went to teacher training at Moray House which was like going back to school in a building that, with its cold yellowing white tiles, resembled a big public lavatory. I got a job at Daniel Stewart's and Melville College, then got promoted there, then got promoted again into a job in pastoral care, then left to be Head of English at George Heriot's. After four years I became Head of Sixth Year, a job I loved; then for ages I was Head of the Senior School. Finally, under unexpected circumstances, I became Principal and I did that for the thirty-nine months leading to my retirement.

I loved my career, and I don't regret a single thing about it. I applied for fourteen posts in my thirty-seven years in teaching, and I got seven of them, though I only ever taught in two different schools. I was very lucky. But I did not get jobs at Dollar Academy or Hutchesons' in Glasgow, or George Watson's College, and the two applications I made to the state sector were (and I think this is bad) not even acknowledged. Sometimes I wonder what my life would have been like if I had taken up a post in a state school right at the start: what would have happened? I was days away from doing that when I was offered my first post. I pretend to myself that it all would have been much the same, but really, who knows? Certainly, during my time as a teacher, independent schools have diverged further from state schools. When I was at school in the Sixties and early Seventies, what happened in state and private schools was much the same, though the facilities and equipment and class sizes might differ. But by 2020, with the advent of Curriculum for Excellence and the greater importance of extracurricular activities in private schools and the difference in disciplinary attitudes between the sectors, there was a bigger distinction in the experience of private and state pupils (or 'learners' in state schools).

But this book is not about education, it's about me and my career in teaching, and not even remotely intended as a primer on the practicalities of classroom practice. I taught as me, as Cam Wyllie, Waz, Willy, Cammy Chameleon, Slim and finally Mr Wyllie, and I do not think that whatever skills I developed would be easily imitated by others. As a senior teacher I watched lots of great lessons being taught by teachers of every subject, and never once thought that they were teaching like I taught; I was often left open-mouthed in admiration of the skills on display, skills which I completely lacked. I have never, ever, done a PowerPoint presentation.

However, one great universal truth for all of us in teaching is that, almost without exception, no one day, no one lesson, matters that much. The brain surgeon sneezes with the scalpel in his hand – not good. The lawyer adds a zero in a will – not good. The minister of religion forgets the name of the deceased; the electrician rewires badly; the policeman restrains someone too forcibly ... In teaching, the benefits, or the damage, come over an extended period. If you are feeling unwell one day, the kids can sit and read; if you lose a set of essays it doesn't really matter (having said that, on Princes Street one day, a man came up to me and asked for his *Hobbit* essay back, which I had failed to return twenty-two years earlier). Of course, the impact of a good teacher – or a bad one – is huge over a longer period of time, and, very occasionally, a teacher will say something or teach a particular lesson that a young person will always remember. But mainly it is a long hard slog by teacher and student together. No one day, no one lesson.

What do you hold in your hand? Teaching is not like building a bridge, which you can then admire in your dotage. It's more like driving a train back and forth from Edinburgh to Glasgow for forty years and then retiring, except that the passengers, some fleetingly, and sometimes forever, remember the driver's name.

The trajectory of my career took me in a circle from my schooldays at Heriot's to my last day there, after twenty-six years of working. It was central to my life at the ages of five and of sixty: thirty-nine years within that glorious seventeenth-century building, beautiful, grey and sometimes – particularly on rainy days – a bit grim, with its unbeatable view of Edinburgh Castle; indeed, sometimes tourists wandered in thinking it *was* Edinburgh Castle, or, more recently, Hogwarts. So, my life has not been much of a geographical journey, as I have always lived and worked in lovely Edinburgh. It is a journey of people, young, old, dead, exuberantly alive, and it is a journey of which I do not regret a single moment.

*

Did I ever think that I would have liked some other career more? Well, all this time my brother was doing very well as a lawyer in the music business. In 1986 he was interviewed for the Glasgow *Evening Times* – they did a colour spread on him in their centre pages as part of a feature about Scots who had done well in the music business. The reporter, who clearly fancied him, gushed praise about his intelligence, his skills, his good looks; none of which, sadly, could be disputed. Still, he was always good to me, supportive of my career and kind when I came out, so in a mildly masochistic gesture I pinned up the article on my classroom wall. I don't really know why.

I had a registration class of twelve-year-olds. One of them, a cheerful, confident wee boy called Grant looked at it early one morning.

'Mr Wyllie, is that your brother?'

'Yes, it is.'

He continued to read then asked, tentatively, 'Are you jealous of him?'

'No, he doesn't have the pleasure of your company.'

Silence, then with a smile, 'I bet he earns twice what you do.'

I laughed. 'Well, actually Grant, I know for a fact that last year he earned seventeen times what I did.'

But is he happy, I thought, is he happy? Well, obviously he is.

But I was still glad I was doing what I was doing.

Then I went to work at Heriot's, where both of us had been as schoolboys – very different boys, but identifiable brothers: blond, blue-eyed, bright – Jimmy just being fifteen inches taller than me and, well, probably proportionately brighter.

At the end of my first year there, the school celebrated June Day, its ceremony to honour George Heriot, the wise Edinburgh jeweller who lent money to King James VI and followed him to London and who, when he died, fabulously wealthy, left his money to create a school for Edinburgh's orphans.

The ceremony over, I proceeded to the staffroom where there were lots of people eating and drinking. Approaching the crowded buffet to fetch myself a vol-au-vent and a macaroon, I found myself standing next to Jean Stenhouse, who thirty-five years before had taught my brother when he was six. Miss Stenhouse had a puckered mouth and a straight back, and must have been by this time about ninety. In my mind she had always been ancient. She was standing selecting choice morsels and popping them in her mouth. I felt I should say something.

'Hello, Miss Stenhouse!'

I was not, to be sure, convinced she wanted to be interrupted at her grazing, but her eyes were bright enough as she scrutinised me.

'You won't remember me . . .' I began.

'Oh, I do remember you. You are Cameron Wyllie. You got Bryan Jonson's job. You are . . .' in case I had forgotten, 'the Head of English.'

I smiled.

She continued. 'I did not teach you but I taught your brother, James. He was a fine boy. So tall for his age. Such a good-looking boy.'

I am five feet ten inches tall, just half an inch shorter than the average height of men in Scotland. I smiled again. She continued. 'He was dux of the school, wasn't he? Were you dux of the school?'

'Ah, no, no, I wasn't . . .'

'He went to Cambridge, is that right? Did you go to Cambridge?'

'No, I went to . . .'

'He studied Law.' She stopped, presumably realising she needn't ask if I had aspired to that particular height of academic success.

By this time, inevitably, I wanted to crush her like a macaroon. Why had I bothered?

And then a splendid thing happened. Moving in for the *coup de grâce*, my ego spread out in front of her waiting for the next thrust, she said, 'What is he doing now?'

'Well, he's done very well. He does a lot of work with pop groups.'

Jean Stenhouse was stilled by this, concerned. She paused, put a tiny sausage roll in her mouth, chewed and swallowed. Then she turned fully to me, placed one hand on my arm and said, 'Well, at least you've done well.'

Young Teacher

A History of History

In 1980, I went on teaching practice to Daniel Stewart's and Melville College, as it was then rather clumsily called. I looked about thirteen, weighed eight and a half stone, and, on the first day, wore a brown three-piece suit, featuring massively flared trousers, which I had bought at a fire sale in Glasgow for £7. I wish I was making any part of that last sentence up. That first day was not a wholehearted success, and I am very grateful to the colleague who suggested that the suit might have been my undoing. I binned it and things got better, though it lived on in the memory of some of the boys rather longer than one might have wished – for perhaps four or five years.

Anyway, I loved DSMC, and the English department was greatly supportive and good fun. They sat and laughed together in the staffroom, always in the same place, really irritating the little closed groups of physicists and mathematicians around them with their cheery loudness, to which I was only too happy to contribute. So I was very pleased when the Head of English, Tom Fraser (called 'Tam' by every soul in the place) suggested I might like to apply for a job there.

The only problem was that the job involved teaching English and History, and I hadn't studied any History at university. In the present day, that would be an automatic no-no, because the General Teaching Council for Scotland runs teachers with an iron fist and academic qualification in the subject they teach is essential, which is, I suppose, fair enough – though I've seen many crap teachers in my time with a Ph.D. Of course there are plenty of exceptions, and one of them was Dr Andrew Tod, the Head of History, uniformly and correctly regarded as a brilliant teacher, who had taken a kindly interest in the seemingly adolescent, fairly camp young man who was the English student (his interest, it should be said, was nothing to do with my being camp, since he was, as everyone who knew him would agree, resolutely heterosexual). Andrew assured me that if my spirit was willing, a bit of weakness elsewhere could be overcome and that if, as he hoped, I got the job, he would be there to support and assist me. In any case, the History would only be a couple of classes of younger kids, dead easy; just read the course ahead of them and sound confident.

The astonishing thing is, I believed him.

In fact, very little preparation proved to be possible, in part because one characteristic of the school at that time was the very late arrival of the timetable (very late one year to the extent that, on the first day, most of the kids tried to go to RE at the same time). So it was only on the day before term started that I realised I was to have two classes of S1 History, two classes of S2 History and an S3 class, starting their first year of O-Grade.

Dr Tod cheerfully answered any questions I had and periodically schooled me in the lessons I was to deliver to the younger boys. Some of these involved film strips, two of which I still recall. One was called 'Britain: The Early Twentieth Century', and as he wound the spool through the projector I attempted, initially with some success, to identify the photographs. Then came a picture of a group of men in the back of a truck carrying guns.

'An Edwardian shooting party,' I hazarded.

'Close, close,' he encouraged, 'but not quite. Early IRA volunteers.'

In the period running up to lunch we looked at another strip unpromisingly named 'Russian Generals of the First World War'. I had the little booklet that came with the filmstrip, and attempted to memorise the names as they appeared. They all looked, of course, exactly the same, baleful and bearded. I returned after lunch to teach the lesson, and found that the booklet had gone. An obliging child put the light out and we started.

'So this is . . . a Russian General of the First World War. Notice his . . . medals. He has obviously done great service to Russia in previous wars. What wars might they have been? Yes, that's right, Kevin. Good. Now, does anyone know this General's name?'

The room was, both literally and metaphorically, shrouded in darkness.

'No? Come on now, you're supposed to have read up on this . . . no, well, it's General Bulkakin, famous for the defence of . . . Minsk. M.I.N.S.K. So let's move on . . .'

Another bewhiskered angry-looking old fellow stared out from the dingy screen.

'Now, does anyone know who this one is? Oh dear . . . that's not very good. This is . . . em . . . General Podovski. He was a General in the First World War. Which other countries were taking part in the First World War? Good, lots of hands.'

I very slowly went round the room, taking answers. Luckily, a great many countries took part in the First World War, and I allowed in some (Brazil) that hadn't, just to make the period run away faster. But eventually I had to move on to a third General, whom I had just christened ('This is General . . . just let me think a minute . . . Keronovsky. Now tell me how many military ranks come before General . . . yes, good, Kevin . . .'), when Dr Tod appeared at the door, briskly asking how the lesson was going, and keen to return the booklet accompanying the pictures, which he had – inadvertently, he claimed – picked up and taken away.

How we laughed. Later.

Essentially, though, teaching History to the younger boys was quite straightforward. I read the textbook. I asked them questions. They wrote things down. The tests were very factual. They did ok. Nobody complained. The Third Year class, who were actually starting work towards a national examination, were, from the outset, a different and more serious prospect.

There were nineteen of them. They ranged from a clever, witty, quiet intellectual who went on to do History at Oxford, to a more ebullient, less academic, curly-headed boy who went on to do six years in Saughton Prison for, I understand, a pretty poor effort at armed robbery. They got my measure very quickly, well before I got theirs. No one actually ever said 'Do you know anything about History?' or 'What you just said is absolute shite', but they knew and it gave them power. They quickly took a liking to me but, to be honest, they had no reason to respect me, so each of these double periods, two a week, was an ordeal to be suffered. Thank God my little classroom was situated close to the staff smoking room (or 'Upstairs Quiet Room' as it was officially known). I would like to thank Mr Benson and Mr Hedges for saving my sanity while shortening my life.

My teaching of them was terrible. While I was planning interesting and innovative lessons for my four English classes, I had, in truth, no idea how to teach History except by telling the class things while they listened and wrote these things down. Except, of course, I didn't know the things. English teaching is a breeze by comparison with teaching anything else, apart from the marking, because English teachers don't really know anything, and have spent their student days reading novels and drinking liqueurs and having sex. But for History it seemed to me to be necessary to know the course. Accordingly, I enlisted the help of my friend Margaret Forwell, a very clever medic, who still had her notes for O-Grade History from eight years before when she had attended St Margaret's School for Girls (pronounced 'Gurls'). So the lesson plan would be that I would more or less dictate Margaret's immaculate, beautifully written notes, spelling the difficult words on the board, for one period, and then we would have a 'discussion' for the second period, which was meant to be based on what they had just written down. There were moments of angst even with the benefit of this precious resource. The Prime Ministership of Lord Rockingham – he was Prime Minister twice, who'd have thought – was summed up in Margaret's notes as 'Lord Rockingham was a colourless man', so I rather cautioned the boys against answering a question on him in the exam.

The discussions, unlike the Second Marquess of Rockingham, were anything but colourless. They had a predisposition towards a discussion of homosexuality. Thus, when I asked 'Who can tell me anything about Palmerston?'

'He was gay.'

'No . . . I don't think so . . .'

'Sir, do you feel anything in common with Palmerston?'

So, quite often the discussions were actually riots, though broadly they stayed sitting down, and very occasionally, when they were really, really bad, I managed to shut them up.

There were games of course. One of the boys was called Hamish. He is a professional actor now. I danced at his wedding. When he was fourteen he was a brilliantly clever, very funny, astonishingly skinny boy and, it transpired, he could imitate pigeons. The boys were alarmingly quiet that day and I was consequently on the alert. A faint cooing seemed to come from somewhere and then one of them said 'Is there a pigeon in the room?' I won't protract the agony, but suffice to say I eventually was looking under my desk for the bird, while they read silently, with, I imagine, tears of joy streaming down their faces.

Once, after break, they locked me out of my classroom. Somehow or other they had all got in before me. I had my key but they had locked the door on the inside. The hectic, noisy corridor subsided into calm and quiet as the other doors shut. Then there was just me, pleading to be let in. At that point, horrifically, Clem Bell appeared some distance away, visible through two sets of double doors, puffing away at his pipe, and, for the moment, oblivious to my increasingly desperate efforts to get into the room and resume my teaching of the Suffragette Movement.

Clem, the Deputy Head, was, from his appearance, made of mahogany; a small, squat, very good man of the old school and as hard as nails. His favourite story was of finding a boy at the school playing fields, carving something into the wood in the changing-room. 'What does that say?' he said, his hand no doubt on the perpetrator's collar. '"Clem is a bas"... now what could that be?'

'Clem is a bastion of the school, sir,' replied the youth. Clem laughed and laughed when he told that story. Still, I imagine the boy was put to death.

Anyway, there was Clem, and there was me in the corridor.

'Mr Bell is coming,' I pleaded through the door.

'No, he's not.'

'Yes, he is. He really is!'

'Everything ok, Mr Wyllie?' said Clem with a hint of suspicion, his nose twitching, smoke wafting from his pipe.

'Yes, indeed, there's something wrong with my key.'

There was a click, a shuffle, and the key turned. The door swung open. There the boys were, silently sitting studying.

'Very good, Mr Wyllie, very good,' said Clem. I doubt if he was actually taken in for a moment, but it could have been a great deal worse.

Years later, unwell, I had to go to the loo during a class, which took about two minutes. When I got back, a child was sitting on the floor clutching his bleeding head, having 'fallen off' his seat. This was a disaster. He went to Matron, and Matron later came to me. There would have to be an accident form, she said, with, I thought, an edge of glee. Well, there was, and I had to see Clem.

'Try not to let it happen again,' he said as he crumpled up the form and threw it in the bin.

And then there was the stick. My predecessor, a young, cheerful and phlegmatic Englishman had left behind a short pointed stick which I became accustomed to carrying while I was teaching. I walked about a lot, and would periodically tap it on a desk to get attention. On one occasion, at the end of a lesson, a group of boys were gathered round my desk and one of them, a particularly smiley small boy called Colin, made a witticism that caused me to tap him on the head with the stick. Except it turned out to be a bit more than a tap and he burst into tears.

This was 1982, and I had been teaching for about six months. I apologised immediately and he stopped crying, but I assumed my career was over. However, this was 1982, when parents didn't have lawyers. Bless 1982 and its different style of parenting, which resulted in a letter the following day from Colin's mother, which I opened with a fake smile and a ton-weight of dread. The letter said that they understood I had hit Colin the previous day. This was, he had assured them, an accident, which had stemmed from my being irritated by his being silly. Mum said that she understood he was a silly boy (he was not) and that she, and Colin's father, wanted to thank me for being his teacher. It must, she said, be very stressful being a young teacher, so Colin and she had baked me a cake, and there indeed in front of me was a most magnificent Victoria sponge, instead of disgrace, imprisonment and the newspapers. Thank you Colin, you cheery soul. I hope you are still smiling somewhere.

Anyway, this stick and I became inseparable, which, of course, led the historians in my care to try to separate us. They devised a game, the rules of which were left on my desk one day at the close of business. The stick had disappeared, because they had hidden it. The rules decreed that it had to be hidden somewhere in the classroom and left undamaged and that clues might be provided in an emergency.

I have always hated losing things. It terrifies me. The loss of my bank card in my sixty-first year made me feel physically sick, until I realised where it must be. But, I thought to myself back then, it can't matter that much if I lose that pointer. I can always get another one. So I started to look. That time I found it fairly easily, certainly more easily than when they hid it behind a poster on the wall. Or when they took up a floorboard. Or particularly when, in a fit of inspiration, they unscrewed the blackboard from the wall and put it back with the stick behind it. That one was not easy. Eventually someone stole the stick, broke the rules and broke the stick. It was left on my desk. I would not need to search for it again. A boy, not one of the historians, made me a new one, varnished and with a proper handle, its end tipped with rubber bands; it was, in its way, one of the most moving presents of my life. Thank you, Yann; your stick is here beside me now. It has weathered these forty years; the rubber bands have perished into a hard lump.

I taught History for only two years, and I survived. Nobody died. Well, I was close at times. I cannot, however, emphasise how terrible my teaching of it was. And yet, and yet . . .

It is my first ever Parents' Night and it is for the Third Year. I, of course, have two classes – a perfectly straightforward English class and . . . the history boys. The former class is taught confidently, knowledgeably and creatively; the latter taught from Margaret's old jotters, interjected with the odd riot, discussions about homosexuality and games with the stick. (This list, I realise, might have been better phrased.)

The parents come, unaccompanied in those less consultative days by their children, and broadly, everything goes surprisingly well. The parents are very kind and smile a lot, including the mother of a boy called David, to whom I can barely speak because of her astonishing similarity in looks to her son, a cheerful and amusing boy who looks like a rodent, with, it turns out, a cheerful mother who looks like a rodent in a hat. Anyway, all is going along fine and then Tommy's mother arrives, looking grim, and I fear the worst.

Tommy is one of my History class, and he is not interested in History. To be fair, Tommy is not interested, I understand, in any of the subjects he studies at school. Tommy, unlike most of his peers, is a normal teenage boy, one who, I have learnt from staff meetings, the grapevine and, most importantly, the 'discussions' so integral to my teaching of history, is interested in motorbikes, clothes and girls. There is a suggestion, heaven forfend, that he might even smoke dope. He has jet-black hair and is very good-looking. In my class, though I don't feel any personal animosity from him, he says very little – though plenty is said about him by the others, often by comparing him with historical figures. He sometimes appears to be asleep in class and on one occasion seemed dead to the world during a test, so I tried to wake him up.

'Come on, Tommy, you need to do this.'

'Aw, fuck off, Mr Wyllie,' was Tommy's response.

I didn't do anything about that, but Tommy is not doing very well and now here is his mother, quite an intimidating figure. I begin to speak, but she interrupts – and these, honestly, were her words: 'Mr Wyllie, I am SO pleased to meet you. Mr Wyllie, you've set History alight for our Tommy. He loves it.'

So, here is the truth, young teachers. Never, ever, make any connection between what a parent says to you, and what is actually happening in your classroom. I was not setting History alight for Tommy, but I was letting him sleep more than my colleagues, and so History was his favourite subject. But thank you, Tommy, and all of you historians, my class who sat O-Grade in May 1982, for not clyping. I wish you all well.

Ozzie at the Theatre and Outside the Club

My Higher English class in 1987 were rough and ready, loud and harmless, good humoured, smiling. I taught them Arthur Miller's play *Death of a Salesman*. At first they found Willy, the salesman of the title, boring but they liked his sporty sons, tossing a ball about and talking about women. They liked it when, pressing a pupil for a development of his ideas, I said, 'Well, Tim, to be honest I don't think my Willy is like your Willy.' In fact, that is probably what they remembered most. (As an aside, this is not quite so bad as a story told by my first boss, Tam Fraser, who says that in teaching a difficult class of soon-to-be school-leavers in a tough school early in his career, he was speaking the part of Macbeth in the classroom when instead of saying 'I have no spur to prick the sides of my intent,' he dramatically intoned 'I have no prick . . .')

My classes tried the American accents, which were at least as good as mine – all my classroom stage voices (Othello, Willy Loman, Shylock, Blanche DuBois) sounded much the same, an approach which proved to be ahead of its time now that casting an elderly Jewish woman as Othello (apparently in order to avoid accusations of discrimination) is de rigueur.

Anyway, I took this same class to the Royal Lyceum Theatre to see a production of *Death of a Salesman*. I was a bit nervous but in fact they behaved really well, to the extent that the woman sitting next to me commented favourably on their cheerful dispositions and politeness. That was until close to the end. Willy is dead (the clue is in the title) and his wife – played by a very distinguished Canadian actress, who was really good – kneels by his grave. The flute plays, the agonised faithful wife bids her fickle and vain but beloved husband goodbye: 'Forgive me dear, I can't cry. I don't know what it is, but I can't cry . . .'

And then, by some horrible electronic mischance, the sound system begins to play radio calls from the taxi rank outside the theatre: 'Taxi to Portobello, Johnson, 13, James Street. Taxi to Niddrie Mains Farm, name's McKitterick, taxi . . .'

The actress, still dignified, carries on – 'Help me, Willy, I can't cry …'

'Taxi for Corstorphine. WX15 – are you nearby?'

Now, to be fair, everyone laughed. It was impossible not to. But, utterly professional, she pressed on. Waves of laughter rolled through the theatre. Then she gave one look at us, and she was trying very, very hard, so we all fell silent.

Then Osmond, popularly known as Ozzie, farted loudly. And the last hopeless refrain of the cast – 'we're free, we're free', as well as the curtain calls (Willy's wife got a standing ovation) saw the audience in hysterics.

A few years later, when that class of boys turned twenty-one and I was moving on from Stewart's Melville, they invited me out for dinner, and about ten of them turned up. We had some Chinese food and went to a club, because they made me. We stood in a line to get in, me and these excessively heterosexual boys, all by this time a bit pissed. Ozzie was there; he was always quite little, cheerful, freckled. He looked about twelve, and the enormous bouncer, eighteen times Ozzie's bulk, would not let him in.

'Aw, come on man,' Ozzie pleaded. 'I'm twenty-one. I've been here *lots.*'

'Move along, son,' said the bouncer.

'Look, ask him,' said Ozzie, earnestly, pointing at me. 'He's my teacher.'

Smukke Piger

Teaching English is mainly an unstructured mess based around texts. Sometimes you have to stop and explain a concept. I used to like to hear older students talking about what literature was – was the telephone directory (that dates me) literature? And it was good, just occasionally, to feel, in the way that teachers of Maths and Chemistry and History must do every day, that students left the room knowing something that they did not know when they entered it. Like, for example, terms for 'literary effects'.

One thing that has always bugged me is the incorrect use of the word 'onomatopoeia'. If you're not careful, twelve-year-olds think it applies to a great many more words than it actually does. So you can tell them about the words 'maluma' and 'takete', which are nonsense words invented for an experiment conducted in the 1920s. You ask the students which word means a balloon and which means a knife, and they will say that 'maluma' is a 'nice' word so it must mean balloon, while 'takete' is a 'sharp' word. So they fit the sound to the word – this is not onomatopoeia.

You can then tell them about the research that shows that the words for the noises cats and dogs make are more or less the same in hundreds of languages, and so these words are onomatopoeic. But my favourite example of how the sound of words can mislead always was 'smukke piger', which is Danish for 'beautiful girls'. Now of course I know that if, nowadays, an inspector watched me teaching a lesson which even hinted towards the beauty of girls I would be burned alive using sustainably sourced wood; but in 1985, I thought that my question to the students was really clever. 'What does "smukke piger" mean?' Dirty, piglike, nasty, mucky, criminal etc. were the translations always offered. No, I would say triumphantly, it is the Danish for 'beautiful girls' and thus what does this tell you about language? That it doesn't usually mean what it sounds like, but on the very rare occasions it does, it's ..? Onomatopoeia! Job done, wha hey! And then I would say that when their mum asked them what they had learned in school that day they should say, 'Mr Wyllie says you're a smukke piger.' (I know, I know, the pyre burns bright, but then again, I think lots of their mums probably realised I wasn't an actual sexual threat.) Of course, these boys had memories which were not like sieves, they were simply one big hole, so they very rarely remembered. However, once in a blue moon . . . 'So, what did "smukke piger" mean? Yes, good, beautiful girls. Anyone tell their mum? You did, Tony? Good, what did she say?'

'Well, I didn't mention you. I just said she was a smukke piger and she slapped me before I could explain.'

Ah, 1985.

Tripping: Wally, Arnold, Vermont

Three years into my time at Daniel Stewart's and Melville College I went to Vermont, in the upper north-eastern United States. I took a group of young people with me – boys from DSMC and girls from the Mary Erskine School up the road. They were lovely kids, ten of them, kind and innocent.

I went to Vermont because of Wally Shaw, the Reverend Wallace Allen Shaw, who was the chaplain at Stew Mel, and who was, quite possibly, the kindest man I ever knew, a liberal Christian who had integrated a white church in his native USA, then left fairly abruptly after that, because integration of the church was not what the elders had had in mind. Wally was a large, silver-haired man with a huge and constant smile, an academic intellectual and a stand-up comic who told terrible jokes, and he persuaded me, without difficulty, to become involved in Operation Friendship.

Operation Friendship came about thus: in the late Sixties Wally had a church in Glenrothes, a 'new town' in Central Scotland, and his church had a lot of poor people in it. Wally, however, was a wealthy man, and he decided that he wanted to take a group of kids from Glenrothes to Indiana for a holiday, so he did. I think some effort at fundraising was involved, but I suspect mainly he paid. So these kids went and had three weeks in this new and loving environment – hosted by a church in Indiana, though Operation Friendship was always fairly light of touch in terms of religion. Anyway they came home, and the next year hosted a much bigger group of Americans. And so on, and it grew, and so on, and it still exists – groups of young people going to the States one year, and groups of American kids coming to Europe (lots of countries) the following year. And this was Wally's brainchild.

So it happened that in 1983 I went to Vermont and stayed with Arnold and Judith in the parsonage beside the white wooden church at Craftsbury Common. Eventually I travelled with OF four times – first to Vermont then, at two yearly intervals, to Columbus, Indiana, to Toms River, New Jersey, and finally, in 1989, to Scituate, Massachusetts.

Every time I stayed in someone's house and they were good to me. I made plenty of friends, young and old, in these real American towns, people showing me and these four groups of kids their hospitality and kindness, the energy and drive of this huge and varied country. But all these years later, I remember Vermont most clearly, lodged as it is, not just in my memory, but in my heart.

I didn't know the first thing about Vermont when I was told we were going there. Truth to tell, I am really a city boy, and in these pre-internet days, the pictures I could see made it look like an awful lot of trees, in most cases laced with an awful lot of snow. I knew people skied there, but it would be summer, and in any case, I had always thought that if God wanted us to ski he'd have given us long wooden feet. Still, I was young and enthusiastic and tried to gee up the kids, made easier when bits of the program for the trip arrived – lots of camping and swimming, and craft activities and . . . a number of things to do with maple syrup, and church. My professional skills were a bit pushed on the last one. OF was organised in churches in the USA and schools in Europe, and I could only find one practising Christian among my group, so he was in charge of providing Scottish prayers.

But we all got excited, and then we went. I remember the light and the heat when we disembarked in Boston airport, and the realisation that I felt really sick. We got into a minibus for the five-hour journey, me in front with the driver Anne, a grand, feisty woman. Very quickly I had to tell her that I was three degrees away from vomiting. But we talked and for a while I thought I was better.

Then we arrived at the Fiorucci Brothers Pizza House, greeted by a huge sign on the freeway. They had, I was told, agreed to give the 'Scots kids' pizza and 'beverages' on the house. I told the kids, who were sleepy and grumpy, to be charming, and we went in – ah, the smell of fresh pizza, cheesy and rich. My goodness, I wanted to puke, but in the men's room I couldn't make myself.

I emerged, pale and clammy, and accepted a Mountain Dew, a luminescent green soda, a gulp of which made me feel yet worse. I hastened outside for some uncheesy air and beside a large wooden structure – actually, it transpired, the sign welcoming us to the Fiorucci Brothers Pizza House – I barfed until I could barf no more, unable to stop even when a carload of concerned nuns drove into the car park, looked at me, then drove out again. I got back in the minibus and slept a relieved sleep. By the time we got to the North East Kingdom of Vermont it was pitch dark, stars shining bright above us, and I was woken from a fractured sleep by a sweet-voiced kid knocking on the window and saying 'Are you the kids from Scatland?' That sweet-voiced kid, Steve, will be touching fifty now, but I can hear him still.

So I woke up and we moved around Orleans County, dropping off the kids to their host families until, at last, Anne took me at midnight to the parsonage beside the church on Craftsbury Common, a dim light above its door, and there was Judith Brown and a big sleepy dog. Judith made me a cup of milky tea. I do not drink tea, and I don't like milky drinks, so my effort to gracefully welcome this first hospitality had a final emetic result. After ten minutes' chat I retired quickly to throw up again, then went to bed, exhausted but no longer sick.

I woke late the next day, drank some water, ate some food, then sat outside on the porch, reading. It was a day of brilliant sunshine, the sky a blue I had never seen before, the air so fresh you wanted to gulp it down. One of the girls in my group rode past on a horse, appearing to my sun-squinty eyes like a vision, and stopping only to say hello before she and her host and new friend rode away. I remember sitting there feeling tremendously well and at peace, a mood that stayed with me for the three weeks to come.

I could tell you so much about the people we met and the things we did there, simple things, swimming in a lake with enormous blue dragonflies for company, having a barbecue, making maple snow out of maple syrup and … snow, brought in from somewhere. I went into a field with a camping stove and ate sweetcorn plucked from the plant. One night towards the end, we were entertaining the community in the church hall with a little show we had hastily prepared before. Everyone came. Earnest and cheerful, Jimmy gave a talk about Scottish architecture, based mainly on the distinction between stone and wooden houses and a set of slides which showed a series of identical Edinburgh homes, 'and here's another stone house'; I read some Burns; Mhairi led the country dancing; we sang 'Flower of Scotland' rather half-heartedly, passed out the words, then everyone sang it lustily, as if, in those five minutes, every Vermonter became a Scottish Nationalist. Then a farmer came and took us to see the Northern Lights in the back of his trailer, in the middle of his field – he was just passing and thought we might be interested. It was one of the most beautiful and strange things I have ever seen, the kids hushed by the intense darkness and nature playing some kind of trick on them.

But really I want to talk about Arnold.

On the evening of the first full day I was there, Arnold and I sat on the porch and talked and this became our custom; each day, after the young people had gone their various ways home through the woods with their host families, we would sit in the gathering gloaming (I taught him that word) and just talk. No booze was involved, for the Browns did not drink – when I had presented Judith with a bottle of whisky from my dad, she said, 'What a beautiful bottle. We'll keep it forever.' After the second night, when I had delayed the talking so I could go for 'a walk round the Common' (a euphemism for smoking a cigarette) Judith simply said, 'See these walks. You can smoke on the porch if you like.' So Arnold and I had plenty of time to talk about things. We talked about God and church, though thankfully he was no missionary; we talked about family (the Browns had four children in total, but only one close by); we talked about Scotland; we talked about popular culture (how, Arnold wondered, could it be right to allow a song called 'Cocaine' to be broadcast); and we talked about politics. This latter led to the only frisson between us, but it was short-lived. Arnold suggested to me that I thought he was right-wing, and I had to agree, then he told me of his work with the Southern Christian Leadership Convention; he had not met Martin Luther King but had conversed with JFK. He had been in the navy in 1945 as a chaplain's assistant. He was, as well as a minister, an immigration inspector and a crack shot, though he said he had never, and could never, actually shoot a gun at anyone. We talked forever, and sometimes Arnold recorded our talks to listen to them again. I would like to think he did that. The only break in our conversations came when the Browns had their friend Howard and his wife to visit from South Dakota, in the middle of my stay. She was a kind person, very quiet; I realised why when Howard joined us on the porch. Arnold liked to talk and I like to talk but Howard outclassed us every time. I loved everything I did in these three weeks but I loved most coming home to the parsonage, to Judith's soothing good sense and Arnold, always up for a talk about more or less anything.

Arnold was the minister of the church, but, as I say, he was also a guard on the border with Canada, and one day the group all went to visit him on duty there. We had our passports stamped, which resulted in those kids, and, shortly after, their many, many friends back home, finding out what my actual first name (George . . . now so fashionable, but then not) was . . . is . . . as Arnold's young colleague on the Canada side passed back our passports. Then Arnold took us into a little house, where the owner, a kindly old lady, showed us her sitting-room in the USA and her kitchen in Canada. The grand finale was her bedroom. She slept, she said, with her feet in Canada and her head in the USA. Then Graham, a boy in our group, said something funny.

And thirty-six years went past. I went to see Arnold again in 2019 at the peak of the Vermont fall, which I had never seen before, always before being a summer visitor. I had not seen the leaves when they are sewn into quilts of colour; as we drove about I gaped as each turn revealed some new miracle of colouring – sometimes a single tree, among others, looking as if it were internally lit, or as if some practical joker had got up in the night to paint each leaf.

When I arrived at the care facility which now looked after him, he was sitting in his wheelchair amid a group of elderly ladies, being read to by a charming young woman. The old ladies seemed less than pleased when Phil, his son-in-law, excused Arnold and wheeled him to his room. There he was: very frail, wholly blind, his hearing impaired but much improved by very powerful aids. He was, in Scottish terms, 'wandered' – this means 'an old person who is rather confused' but

chastened into submission by whichever Chemistry teacher had been suborned into taking that bottom group. If the ball came near us we moved towards it very slowly, only because actively running away from it – our natural instinct – might actually be regarded as revolution. We did not tackle, of course, and feared being tackled. My God, what was it all for?

So it was with some alarm that on starting to teach at DSMC, I was assigned to a rugby practice. To coach it. To be in charge. This came about after a conversation with Robin Morgan, the Principal, in which, in his straightforward manner, he said that debating (which I knew a lot about) was really for girls and that it would be necessary for me to take a rugby practice. When I said that I didn't even know the rules, he looked at me rather sharply and said 'I think you mean the laws . . .'

The school provided me with rugby boots and with a vivid nylon tracksuit in which my resemblance was less to a rugby player than to a specialist rent boy. And it provided me, more usefully, with Gilbert Parkhouse. Google Gilbert and you will read of his very distinguished career in cricket playing for Glamorgan and England – another great sportsman poached for England, though I don't even know if there is a Welsh cricket team. Apparently he could 'on-drive' beautifully, whatever that means. He had, extremely unusually, also played rugby for Swansea.

By the time I met him he was fifty-five, but seemed a great deal older. He had been, in one of the Scottish private school sector's efforts to be the English private school sector, DSMC's 'cricket professional', and now was the librarian. Gilbert's favourite books were the immaculate collection of copies of Wisden's annual cricket almanac. He maintained silence in the library, read the paper, then turned to Wisden. He had broken two club records in 1950 but he never spoke to me about his own sporting past. He was a gentleman, and he did his best with little wet me and I think, in the end, he quite liked me. He held court from a chair at the end of the table on the far side of the staffroom, in which anyone else sat at their peril, and he smoked and smoked and smoked.

On term time Mondays, for two years, Gilbert would drive me to Inverleith to take the bottom practice in Second Year, a group which varied in size according to how many of them managed to skive on any one occasion, but which peaked at about fifty, being all the boys not in the top four teams, which were left in the hands of more experienced teachers, some of them actually qualified. Gilbert probably knew more about rugby than the rest of them put together, but, in the way of great sportsmen, he hirpled about, his hips and knees having 'gone', and thus became what he described, nobly, as my 'assistant'. As we drove, Gilbert, having seen that any effort to engage me in learning about rugby was doomed, talked about his favourite things – red wine, good steak, travel and, on occasion, pretty women. I am sure he never actually strayed from Mrs Parkhouse, but he was always encouraging my interest in one or other of the female staff, and I did not think it wise to enlighten him that I played for the other team in that particular stadium. His chat was great, he shared my interest in gossip, and there was time for two Bensons each before we got there. One when we set off, prior to actually starting the car, and one when we reached the lights at Telford College, when he would force another upon me. In winter, we arrived smoked, and this, as you can imagine, set me up very well for the afternoon's running about 'coaching' the sweet-natured, plump, skinny, very clever, extremely stupid, girly, sensible, weird children who found themselves in the apartheid slum of the bottom practice.

I had very little idea of what I was doing. I grasped some basic notions – the ball could not, for some reason, be thrown forward, even though the entire object of the game was to get it forward; it was not manly to stop someone by heaving at their body, but it was manly to throw yourself at their feet; scrums were dangerous, so you put a hooker in the middle, and then everyone pushed their faces more or less against everyone else's bum. Of course most of our boys, just like Colin and I ten years before, didn't want to do any of that, and I couldn't blame them. But Gilbert stood smoking at the side of the pitch, occasionally having changed into a tracksuit of great antiquity, but most of the time in a black jacket and club tie, his library uniform, and we were all a little afraid of him so we did what we had to do. I had made him accept one condition of my servitude as a novice rugby coach – if rain fell, we stopped play. So it was that on many a Monday my enormous squad of sporting refugees hurtled back to the changing-room because of a little moisture, unmanly but happy.

Gilbert had a whistle and I had a whistle. Broadly, he stayed still and I ran about, maintaining a semblance of control. On many occasions, however, Gilbert was unable to control his irritation at the wholesale parody of his second favourite game which I was allowing to happen. He would blow the whistle and, smiling, say 'Mr Wyllie, I think you may have missed a knock-on [I had no idea really what one looked like] about three minutes ago.' One time, excited by the gathering clouds, and particularly wheezy due to the combination of tobacco and incipient asthma, I failed to notice that the two teams had, on Gilbert's instruction, changed ends. The Reds touched the ball down, behind what was, in fact, their own line. 'Try to the Reds!' I shouted, authoritatively.

The Blacks, not unreasonably – well, those of them who gave a toss – gathered around me noisily, complaining. While I tried to make sense of what they were saying, Gilbert more or less ran from the side, and shoved the complaining Blacks away, bouncing some of them off the ground.

'Penalty to the Reds, penalty to the Reds,' he declaimed, cuffing the back of some child's head. 'Blacks arguing with the referee.'

Silence fell.

'Boys, under no circumstances must you ever argue with the referee, do you understand?'

Then he took my head in an armlock, and leaning down, whispered with affection, 'even when he is a bloody idiot'.

And then he laughed and laughed.

Gilbert is long dead. When I think of him I think of the glow of a cigarette as the first dark fell in the autumn, a gold tooth glinting as he smiles at yet another terrible sporting solecism performed by useless skinny me, and I thank him.

Adolf

In 1986, for reasons still unclear to me, the school granted me permission to go on a jolly to the USA, on the pretext of chaperoning a group of lovely kids who were taking part in a trip organised by the English-Speaking Union. They came from all over Scotland, were clever, well-behaved young people whose Higher examinations I had to invigilate (or 'proctor' as they say in the States) in a hot, dusty American classroom while we were away. Weird planning, but not my weird planning. It was a very easy trip, based in New York State in the town of Schenectady (the Mohawk word for 'beyond the pines'); we all stayed in homes with local families, and mine was delightful. There was a Ben and Jerry's close by and my hostess made iced tea of great merit. All in all, it was a lovely skive, and all the better as it ran for three weeks of term.

Back at the ranch, my classes were being taken by a nice old lady who had been brought in to cover. She was tiny and retired, and, as I packed my sun-cream and T-shirts, I gave half a thought to her well-being. I had, of course, briefed her prior to departure. She had sat with me in the staffroom, intently taking notes, while I described my classes. I had warned her about my rambunctious, cheerful, fairly rough Fourth Year class – a lot of sportsmen, big boys who took up a lot of room and of whom there were many, the next to bottom set. I told her they had taken time to tame but were now entirely on side, just be a bit stern at first. However, I said, the really difficult class was the top set in Third Year, every lesson a bit of a negotiation with these kids, who were clever – some of them brilliantly so – a bit effete, many of slight stature, maybe occasionally a tiny bit slapped about because of their smart mouths; I empathised with them – I had been that wee poof who couldn't shut up – but I did not find them easy. Take care, I said, they may flatter to deceive you.

So off I went on my trip and returned three weeks later. My colleagues were pleased to see me, for it became clear that my absence had required them to do extra work, a state of affairs for which I suffered the rest of that long summer term, even agreeing to take part in a Staff/Boys cricket match to recompense them. The old lady had been rather needy, it transpired; the vitality, bad language, boisterousness and general horseplay (ah, horseplay . . .) of an all boys' school in 1986 had proven a bit much for her. My boss grimly briefed me, unimpressed by the American sweeties I had bought at the airport, and then I went to see the old lady herself. She seemed even smaller than a month earlier.

I had been wrong, it transpired. The Fourth Year class had been terrible, uncontrollable: 'Mr Fraser had to come in several times'; this I knew, for Mr Fraser had made the point to me himself. Some of these harmless big boys had been punished. Their work was awful, late, rushed. She named the worst offenders, many of them particular pals of mine; I frowned supportively and expressed my full intention of expressing my disappointment to them at the earliest possible opportunity (I had no intention of doing this).

But I was also wrong about the Third Year, who had been 'delightful'. 'What a contrast,' she said. 'Such gentlemen. So polite and good-humoured and such lovely work.'

'Well, they are the top set,' I said. 'Their work should be very good.' Gosh, I thought, maybe they have been better with her. Maybe it's me . . .

'So,' I said, 'which pupils particularly impressed you? I will gladly praise them when I see them.'

'Well,' she said thoughtfully, 'they were all very nice, but there were one or two who went out of their way to be welcoming. I particularly liked Adolf.'

My heart leapt with joy. There was, of course, no child named Adolf in the class. I have never taught an Adolf. It seemed scarcely credible she had believed it. But Adolf, I knew who you were.

'Adolf, yes, Adolf,' I murmured. 'You know, it's been a month. Does Adolf have red hair, and a constant smile?'

'Yes,' she said proudly, obviously thinking that she now knew them better than me.

'And he sits next to . . .' I screwed up my face, as if trying to remember.

'Donald,' she said.

'Donald?' I queried (no Donalds either).

'Yes. Donald Dick.'

Donald Dick. Adolf. Then Felix, Clark Kent, Wang Po (there were no Chinese boys in the class) etc. The original class list had been 'mislaid' (filched, I am in no doubt) and here was a list with the marks for their short stories. And here were the short stories.

The short stories were, indeed, beautifully written. They had been given a loose theme to do with 'someone getting something that they really wanted'. In one, Miranda, a teenage girl, had always wanted to play the flute, and had, for her birthday, been given a long pink flute, which she enjoyed taking to her pouting lips. It made her SO excited ...you get the picture. Most of them were thinly disguised adolescent filth, which the old dear had totally missed. There was, in truth, no point in punishing the boys, although I did initially threaten them. I felt bad enough about it without having them hate me too.

Adolf. Oh, Adolf. One of the funniest pupils I ever had, and a tiny bit crazy. I will not name him, for he will now be a QC or an international drug dealer, or writing advertising copy in New York, doing one of these things, many of them wonderful and some of them useless, which very clever boys from Stewart's Melville went on to do. I liked him, but he was really a devil. One of his ploys involved phoning the Open Line Show, which was a radio phone-in programme broadcast between 11 pm and 1 am on a Saturday night on Radio Forth. This was an institution in the Eighties in Edinburgh, not least because one of the hosts was 'Father Andy', a Catholic priest, who (heaven forfend) was quite nice to gay people and pregnant teenagers, as well as the more frequent callers, women who had just been battered by their drunk men in from the pub. Despite this serious content, it was, at times, very funny, particularly listening to Andy and his co-hosts trying to get the inebriated off the line ('We seem to have lost Hamish, but I hope everything goes well at Powderhall tomorrow ...') and often very moving.

I got onto this late, but Adolf was a frequent caller, each time adopting a new guise. I only heard him once, when he was pretending to be a ninety-seven-year-old woman whose parents had perished on the *Titanic*, and who was phoning to complain about the prospect of 'their final resting place' (in a tremendous Morningside old lady voice – 'thir faaanhal resting plaaaace') being disturbed, a project suggested in the news at the time. Given that I knew Adolf was making a habit of this, it didn't take me long to guess it was him, but this time he was given away by his friends guffawing in the background when he returned once too often to a fairly detailed discussion of his deceased progenitors' 'sea-tossed bones'. The old lady disappeared abruptly and Andy was moved to say, his voice full of genuine disappointment, 'Well, we've lost Deirdre, but to be honest it's sad when people waste our time . . .' making me feel guilty for giggling along to Adolf.

Adolf – wherever you are, I hope you, and Donald Dick and Felix and Wang, are not in jail and are doing well.

SEB

The worst job I ever did in my entire career was mark papers for the Scottish Examinations Board. Teachers claim they do this because they want to examine the national standards, and be exposed to other methodologies and pedagogical techniques, so they can engage more fully in reflecting on their own professional development. This is a fat lie: they do it for cash. They like an extra lump of income just before the summer holidays; it is often the means by which they have an actual summer holiday at all, a week in Crete paid for by sweating over endless Physics or History papers. It is grindingly horrible, and it was particularly so for English teachers starting out as markers in the Eighties. They had the doom-laden privilege of marking Paper 1 and Paper 2 of Higher English for 300 students, thirty envelopes of ten candidates each, in alphabetical order, from thirty diverse schools throughout the nation, all created on the same day in stuffy school halls from Shetland to Dumfries. For each candidate, therefore, I had to mark one essay (35 marks), one Report writing task (excruciating, 15 marks) one long Interpretation (40 marks, and a peculiarly Scottish way of examining English, unreplicated in the exams of any other corner of the Anglophone world) and a short Interpretation

(10 marks). This last task often asked questions about a little light-hearted piece, meant, no doubt, to gladden the hearts of the examinees and cause them to laugh merrily, just at the moment they were poised to commit hara-kiri with their leaky Biro.

If you got into some kind of stride it might be possible to mark one candidate's responses in about twenty-five minutes. I kept a discipline of allowing myself a cigarette after two candidates had been dispensed with; it was a dangerous practice to consume much alcohol, however, because not only did you have to grade the things, you had to add up the marks and record them on various bits of paper of different hues. This part of the process was generally deemed to be something at which English teachers did not excel and, in fact, a set of old ladies was apparently kept in a cupboard at the SEB and brought out each year for the specific task of checking the arithmetic of English graduates.

You were meant to write a brief comment on the essay to explain your mark. 'Thin' was good for an essay commanding 18 marks out of 35 and 'Worthy' for 22. I cried once only – my tears staining an essay from a mature candidate at college, which told of her fraught relationship with her daughter. She was a widow and it had not been easy; she was doing Higher English at the same time as her girl, because she wanted to support her in a subject both of them found difficult. It was beautiful, in lovely handwriting, immaculate in its spelling and punctuation. 35 out of 35. I wrote 'Made me cry', lit a B and H and pressed on. However, you also liked a weak candidate, particularly someone who left out half the questions in the Interpretation, or sometimes just didn't bother doing it at all, or wrote 'I can't do this' or 'This is shite'. It didn't happen often, but I didn't report it when it did, because I was getting my £2.17 for their paper anyway.

One slight saving grace was the markers' meetings, which were long and boring, but which afforded the opportunity to meet and talk to other English teachers and for which one was given a paid day off. The markers were mainly either young (poor) teachers or retired (poor) teachers, and during these meetings they examined in detail a number of scripts which had been sent out to them earlier, and which they had already marked in preparation for the 'setting of exam standards'. We sat together in a lecture theatre in downtown Glasgow with a commonality of spirit akin, I imagine, to those arriving for the first time in prison.

These meetings were conducted by the 'examiners', practising teachers themselves, promoted through the ranks of markers over a period of years. Some of them were the exalted 'setters' who actually prepared the papers, years before, then sent them to be locked in a vault for eventual use. They spent long days closeted together deciding on the marks for a few papers, and clearly having a big laugh. They frequently made private jokes, which were clearly obscure references to shared details of literature, their personal lives and their knowledge of Higher English candidates' work over the ages, so they would say things to each other like, 'Come on, Archie, this candidate's not as bad as the Coatbridge Lady Macbeth' and we all smiled, though locked out of any understanding. There were some amusing stories – one lassie had written her critical essay on her own dad's terrible poems; another very clever boy had made up a Norman MacCaig poem which he called 'Dead Donkey', which sounds exactly like the title of a Norman MacCaig poem to me.

So they were a bunch of jolly old coves, cheerful and often a bit plump, in my day almost all men, and they sat in front of their cowed audience of mere teachers like prophets who knew the secrets of life, rather than merely the correct marking code for question 13 (a). They believed the process of allocating a mark to an essay was an exact science, and they made it clear that those of us who couldn't achieve this level of understanding would be swiftly consigned to the pit of despair, where they could kiss goodbye to a fortnight in Rethymnon.

At my first meeting I was appropriately intimidated by the examiners, but was taken in hand by a very lovely older lady, a Glaswegian, who was called Mrs Tortellini, or Mrs Linguine, or something – so I think of her, all these years later, as Mrs Pasta. She would, she said, keep me right.

The examiner began, 'Now let's look at exemplar 5, the essay about collecting keyrings. I think the team felt that, while this wasn't very promising material, it was a relevant response to question 8, which asks for a detailed description of something that means a lot to you. Now in your preliminary marking you'll have come across a number of essays on this question – most of which deal with the candidate's grandparent or at least some memento of them, or a sporting event, or the tickets for the Osmonds concert their dad was taking them to on the day he had his heart attack. The team was very glad he recovered.' Pause for a laugh.

'Anyway, we thought long and hard about this essay and we came back to it a number of times' (a concept that the audience found unlikely at £2.17 a throw) 'because we couldn't decide if it was category II or category III. But eventually' (he continued, as if announcing the result of the Miss World competition live to 235 million viewers) 'we decided on a mark of 25 and a half marks out of 35. 25. Twenty-six is ok, and 25, but we think those are where the parameters lie. Ok?'

Disaster. I had given it 24, because I had missed the sophisticated use of the dashes in the second paragraph, and had merely thought it very, very dull, if competent. I looked to Mrs Pasta for succour, but she, oblivious to my need, was nodding vigorously and smiling at the examiner. Then she rubbed out the 16 she had awarded the essay and carefully wrote '25' on the sheet. This made me feel much, much better and, I assure you, I made sure she knew I knew. She wasn't quite so cordial after that.

Robin, Gin, Fags

My first Head at Stewart's Melville was Robin Morgan and I really liked him, despite the Luger pistol he kept in his desk and which he occasionally showed to prospective pupils, wide-eyed eleven-year-old boys charmed into coming to DSMC by the prospect of seeing Nazi memorabilia. For Robin was charming, old school, posh, funny – an ex-army officer and a historian; he liked shooting, fishing, attractive women, good wine and amusing conversation. He disliked boring people and was always looking for the next laugh. On one occasion he left a meeting of the whole staff, saying he was going to walk his dogs. As the Deputy Head trundled on, we could all see Robin in the distance walking round the grounds. He was also Principal of the all-girls Mary Erskine School, where some of the more venerable spinsters didn't much care for him. Mind you, they didn't like boys much either.

His wife Fiona was a delight and he adored her. They had endless children. Once I was involved in a production of Benjamin Britten's *Noye's Fludde* (I have no idea why) where our young boys formed the chorus and the talents from St Mary's Music School sang the leads. Robin asked me what I made of the kids from SMMS.

'Oh,' I said. 'Polite and precious and all blessed with silly names ... like Rupert.'

'Like my second-born son,' he responded, only slightly grimly.

In my first year of teaching I taught thirty-five periods a week (today's probationer teachers will assume this is a misprint) and, as you'll remember, many of these were History classes and I wasn't actually qualified to teach that. I inevitably crumbled a bit as time went on, and Robin was drafted in to take a particularly difficult S2 History class for one period a week. This class was a nightmare. It included a boy known as Bod and his friend Jimmy: amiable enough, but dangerous, not exactly keen on the Industrial Revolution, and they took up about half my time, while the other twenty-six, many of them called Mickey, made a lot of noise. On the day that Robin was coming, the class assembled after break and I had to be there at the start. Robin was always late, and the boys sensed my discomfiture as I waited for the Principal to arrive. They would muck about until, ten minutes in, he would arrive. This went on for a number of weeks, then Robin asked to see me.

'They seem very straightforward to me,' he observed mildly.

'I think that might be because you are the Principal, Robin,' I suggested. And I am a skinny twenty-three-year-old vaguely camp wee poof, I didn't add.

'They seem pretty interested in the work,' he continued.

'Well,' I said, and I admit to a tiny smidgeon of exasperation in my tone, 'I think that's because you've been spending the lessons discussing the Malayan Emergency, in which you served, rather than discussing the details of the career of Disraeli, which is currently what S2 are doing. Malaya is not in the exam they are sitting on Tuesday.'

Kay More, Robin's secretary, who dealt with his occasional temper and other excesses with a mild good humour perhaps brought from the golf courses where she spent her leisure time, used occasionally to appear at my door. 'Mr Wyllie, could I have a word?' she asked in her quiet, velvet tones. I scurried outside, fearing I had been found out and my career was over, but no, Robin wanted a fag, or preferably two, if that was ok. I handed over a couple of my B and H (I favoured those golden packets of ten), often my last ones. But I didn't mind, for his propensity to cadge fags was not typical of Robin's otherwise very generous spirit. This was best illustrated by the liberality with which he added vodka to the punch at the Sixth Year Christmas dance. I once got so drunk at one such event that I walked home looking like a hunchback, staring at the ground and mumbling. At another Christmas dance, my partner for the night, my flatmate Angeline, came dressed in an actual ball gown, peach in hue, and Robin appeared the instant we arrived. 'Hello, dear,' he said, to an entirely unfazed Ange, who was noticing that she was the only woman there in an actual ball gown, 'we must dance later. You don't want to spend the entire night with a boring intellectual like Cammy.' Robin, my mother and my Gran were the only people to ever call me 'Cammy', and Robin was the only person ever to call me an intellectual.

Anyway, one morning in about 1986, by which time I was a fairly established teacher, I was walking along the bottom corridor at DSMC, where the offices were, and Robin was standing outside his office, as if waiting for someone.

'Cammy, are you going to teach?' he asked.

I was in fact free for the next two periods, so Robin ushered me into his office, all wood, relics and foreign armaments.

He wanted to talk about a number of things, including discipline, the staffroom and his mother-in-law. It was just after Christmas, during which the lady had irritated her son-in-law; he needed a friendly face to give vent to his feelings. It was about 11.30 am, so Robin suggested a gin and tonic. I didn't really drink gin, but it seemed rude to refuse.

As with vodka, Robin had a generous hand with the gin, and since there was a great deal more gin in his office than tonic, and no ice, the drinks mainly consisted of raw Gordon's. I had probably had my usual cheese and onion roll for break, several black coffees and several cigarettes, but I drank away. We talked and talked, and soon an hour had passed and it was time for lunch. Robin asked Kay to bring in some sandwiches . . . and a bottle of white wine. Of course, by 1.15 pm, we had discussed more or less everything, not that I can remember any of it, smoked all my fags and I was utterly, utterly pished.

With a curious mix of dread and confidence I stumbled up to Room 21, my beautiful classroom with its splendid view of Fettes College, to take the Third Year. I had, I am sure, no concept of what I was supposed to be teaching them. *To Kill a Mockingbird*, probably, but that day the mockingbird was sitting firmly on my shoulder, cawing white noise. So I pulled my chair round to the front of my desk, and said to the students, 'Ask me any question you want.' Thus the lesson went on for eighty minutes, after which I dragged my insensate carcass home and forgot all about it.

Months passed and Third Year Parents' Night came. I liked parents, I knew their sons well, I talked, I charmed, I amused . . . and then an odd thing happened. I did the usual chat to one couple, and then the dad asked if he could speak to me alone. This usually signalled that a) the parents were divorcing, b) one of them was ill, or c) they had run out of cash and needed advice on the fees.

But no.

'Mr Wyllie,' he said, 'Fraser really enjoys your lessons, but one day a while back, he came home and said he thought you might have been drunk.'

I remembered Robin's gin and smiled nervously.

'No, I don't think so. I might have been unwell. Some medication disagreed with me for a while . . .'

'Oh, I'm sorry,' said this kindly man, 'but I think you just sat and talked to them about yourself and your views and things, and answered their questions.'

I tittered. 'Oh yes!'

'Anyway, what you said meant a lot to him, and I really wanted to thank you.'

Then he stood up and left.

And I don't have any idea what I had said, but I guess and fear.

Robin is ninety-one this year, and much the same. Happy birthday, Principal!

Tripping: The Horrible Bus Driver

Why do teachers allow themselves to go on school trips? Obviously, it's to enable young people to broaden their understanding of other cultures and languages; to let them experience aspects of the curriculum they are studying in the raw; and about 457 other educational reasons. Some of this is true. Parents like school trips – having children away from home means they can go on holiday themselves, or enjoy boozy dinners, or have sex. Their kids become someone else's joy and worry. Teachers are *in loco parentis*, which, I suppose, translates as 'being your mad parent'. It does make you think about parental responsibility when you're on a school trip, particularly with older students. How parents spend twenty-four hours a day minding their sons and daughters, making sure, for example, they never drink or smoke a cigarette or have sex; making sure they are always in bed by 10.30; making sure that if they show the slightest sign of illness, they are seen by a doctor (not, ever, offloading them to school when they are bleeding from their ears). Actually, school trips would be a whole lot more fun for all concerned if teachers were actually just doing what parents do – 'Hey son, is that you home? How was the Empire State Building? Did you get anything to eat? There's a banana in the fridge. Your substitute mother and I have just been at a gin-tasting in Harlem. It was *really* good. Can you get yourself up in the morning?'

Sometimes, particularly when they're young, a teacher might think of a trip as a sort of holiday, like a family holiday, except with mum, dad, granny and their thirty kids, some of whom will have allergies, medications, odd bowel habits, phobias, weird eating preferences ('he only eats crackers and chocolate spread': well, madam, that didn't last long) and curious noisy episodes in the night. They are not family holidays – at their best they are memorable, warmly fuzzy, life-enhancing times away with your pals; honestly a school trip where the kids behave is a heart-warming thing. But a bad trip – which can so easily happen – is a fraught nightmare. I was, I think, pretty lucky.

If you are travelling by coach, you need a good driver. By 'good' I don't mean someone who drives particularly well, though that helps; and I don't mean someone who, from the outset, sees themselves as another teacher, because that is problematic, particularly where alcohol is involved. I mean someone who is helpful, flexible, knowledgeable (always useful if they know that France is north of Spain, for example) and who doesn't entirely hate children. Most of them, honestly, are great – shy men, often of a girth redolent of pies, who have driven hundreds of thousands of miles and who understand their importance and their role. But a bastard driver is not a good thing.

So very early one morning we were assembled in the car park at Daniel Stewart's and Melville College, with a large bunch of excited thirteen-year-old boys who were going on a trip to Paris. I was there because I had been asked by Eileen Elder, whom I both liked and respected. She was an actual intellectual, but managed to be a great teacher, partly because she was very funny and partly because she did not suffer fools gladly, or indeed at all. Looking back, it does seem odd that I was waiting there, because I don't speak any French, and indeed think French a slightly silly language, all ooo's and uuu's and wee shrugs and funny faces. However, I was jolly and energetic (this was 127 years ago) and most of the kids liked me (with just a few hating me, which is a pretty fair situation to be in). I was no disciplinarian, but Eileen was in charge, so that would be fine.

So the bus arrived, driven by Bastard (I would like to think that was his actual name, but it was certainly his given name, because after about two hours, that was the name we gave him).

We knew we had done badly in the driver lottery after about ten minutes. Barely at the city limits he drew the bus to a halt in order to chastise a child who, with that middle-class privileged elitist conceit and complacency and supercilious condescension towards working people which we all associate with every child at any private school anywhere, had shut the curtain on his window.

'Who told you you could do that?' shouted Bastard, at the shrinking boy in front of him.

But Eileen was on to this. She knew this was a challenge. 'Why can't he?' she asked mildly.

Bastard, bulky and thick, turned. 'Because the curtains are not to be interfered with. They're decorative.' The curtains were like black plastic wings from a nightmare. 'And this is my bus. They need to do what they're told.'

'No,' said Eileen. 'I think the curtains are to keep the light out. It's ok,' she said, to the general population, and, moments later, the curtains were being closed, all over Europe.

Bastard responded by barely speaking to any of us again. He was difficult and angry. Eventually Eileen had to tell him to stop giving orders to the children. He did it again and she phoned his boss. Then we went for dinner in Paris.

As we stopped, Eileen casually remarked to Bastard that she didn't think parking would be allowed at the spot at which he had halted. Bastard suggested in response that there was a car parked there, and 'if the frogs can do it, I can'. We went upstairs to one of these places that serves three courses of indifferent food very quickly to school groups. I almost remember the lumpy soup I was contemplating when the dimly lit room was filled with flashing blue lights. Below, our bus was surrounded by, not one, but three police motorbikes. Eileen responded politely but negatively to Bastard's suggestion that she accompany him to parlay with said frogs, and we waited for his return with a mix of pleasure in his discomfiture and apprehension lest our bus be towed away.

'They want 2,000 francs now,' he reported, ashen-faced.

'I will phone your boss and get it for you,' Eileen said cheerfully. 'In the meantime, give them this,' handing him a chunk of what was known as 'the float' or 'emergency money', which quite often, in the distant past, became staff booze money towards the end of the tour.

He didn't become a whit nicer, but we just forgot about him until the long, long, long drive back, which inevitably featured a stop just off the Dover ferry at a hideous motorway service station. This had a name like 'The Old Black Bull', and it was just the wrong time in the biological day to be feeding thirteen-year-old boys the wrong kind of sausages, which had probably been made some time before from the old black bull itself. It was about 10 pm when we boarded the bus for an all-nighter back to Edinburgh.

After the ritual threats, the exhausted weans shut the accursed bat flaps and slept; the staff settled at the front, each with the luxury of a double seat. Hours of uneasy troubled doze passed; then in the corner of my consciousness, I heard the time-honoured noise of a child retching. There was a toilet on the bus, so I thought, well, he'll be in there, give it a minute. But then came the sound of someone moving up the bus, then pausing, I think to select which of us, with our eyelids now tightly glued up, he should wake. Well, I was there to be the nice one, so it was me. The kid was a really lovely, kind boy and I felt guilty as I pretended to wake up.

'I'm really sorry, Mr Wyllie, but Mark's been really sick.'

'In the toilet?' I asked, though I knew it wasn't so, because the sick smell had started.

I rose. I thought about waking one of the other teachers, but they were now all pretending to be dead and there wasn't any point. Mark, another very good boy, was right at the back, sitting like a waxwork covered in puke. His friend kept apologising, as if he was the sausage manufacturer.

Now, I am not brave, I am not strong, I would probably run away rather than be any kind of hero, but, ladies and gentlemen, throughout my teaching career, I was always pretty good about sick. I was good at Carbisdale Castle when a girl called Jane vomited into her climbing boots and all the butch mountain men fled. I was good when a fat boy called John vomited onto the colleague I was sitting beside on another ill-fated bus: the colleague had told him twice not to eat any more. In the presence of sick, always remember: breathe through your mouth, and think happy thoughts.

Having ascertained that Mark was alive, I told both of them to stop apologising, gave him a drink of water, got the pal to fetch some fresh clothes from his case (well, freshish, it had been a week, and they were boys). Then I led Mark to the tiny toilet, into which he was followed by his pal, in a true act of friendship, to 'help him'. I believe John Paul II was sanctified for curing a French nun miraculously from Parkinson's, but he didn't go into a tiny space with his pal covered in sick and emerge ten minutes later with a cleaned-up friend in fresh clothes and a plastic carrier bag of vomity ones, did he? So, Nick, wherever you are now, I baptise you Saint Nick of Barf. I relieved this kindly child of his bag of gunky clothes, told the two of them to go to sleep and quietly made my way back up the silent but smelly bus to speak to Bastard.

'One of the boys has been sick,' – as if he didn't know – 'and we need to get rid of these clothes. Can you stop a minute? Or slow down and open the door and I will just chuck them off?'

'Nah,' said Bastard, without even bothering to mention the law, the Highway Code, the company's regs, just nah.

'Ok, I'll just leave them here,' I said, depositing the smelly bag right beside him. He said something but I had vanished into the darkness.

Morning broke, in misty Scotland. The bag had disappeared, clearly thrown off by Bastard when the odour grew too much. Eileen awoke and I reported on the night's events. She took a vote among the four staff as to whether Bastard should get the standard £50 tip she was carrying; after a brief campaign the result was a landslide for 'No'. However, the kindness of children is such that they would have become attached to Bastard even if he had been Himmler. The same Nick, bless, appeared beside us and asked if he could take up a collection 'for the driver'. We agreed, knowing full well that the kids would have no money left, and, indeed, as the bus rolled into the school car park around 7 am, with the sleepy parents duly assembled in their big cars, I was able to ascertain that the little paper bag of the collection contained £1.47 in very small change. Pleasingly, it felt more than that in the hand. Nick even gave a brief speech of thanks, there was a tiny bit of applause (less than a smattering, I would say) and we got off.

Eileen, usually so precise and strong with the kids, had accidentally forgotten to give them the usual 'there will not be a single bit of litter left on this coach' routine, and the undersized and useless plastic bags Bastard had provided were overflowing. So we left him in his clarty, smelly bus, and I never saw a coach driver like him again.

Long John

When I started teaching, I liked my First Year classes best, and I expect a lot of new teachers experience the same feeling – twelve-year-olds are fresh and chatty and enthusiastic and, most importantly, broadly speaking do what they are told. Weirdly, this happens again in Sixth Year; in between lies adolescence and its admixture of hormones, fear, bad skin, social media, actual hard exams, not speaking to anyone in your family except your granny, too much porn, more fear, drugs – alongside all this, teachers can seem a bit of an encumbrance. But the First Years are fun, and the Sixth Years have learned, they have survived. Of course, as time passes and you realise you can actually teach say, S4, so that they pass exams and are happier people, the urgent necessity of helping adolescents survive the world can become a teacher's ruling passion, but the First Years are always a bit of light relief.

My first First Year class was unique for me because I taught them English and History, so I saw them six times a week. By Christmas, I would have adopted them all, though it would been a crush at home. They will be fifty-two now, and I remember them all. The day before the Easter holidays was the first of April; at the end of the lesson I said, 'Ok, I hope you have a good holiday. I have been asked, before you go, to give you your exam timetable.'

The First Year did not have exams.

'Well, I'm telling you now, aren't I? Come on, get your homework diaries out. Now, the first thing is that the School Hall's availability is quite limited in Term Three, so your first exam, which is your English exam – why is the first exam your English exam? Yes, that's right, Simon, because English is your most important subject – anyway, we can't do it actually during term so it will be on the day before you come back, which is Sunday the 17th of April, so write that down. You need to be in school for 9 am that morning. Well, sorry, Brian, you'll have to see if you can come back from Tenerife early. Ok, so that's the English exam 9 am to 12 o'clock, then a break for lunch, then 12.15 to 3.15. To be honest, I'm not sure, Mickey, Mr Fraser hasn't told me, but an essay, I'm guessing, and an Interpretation, and maybe, writing a poem or something. Anyway, the next day is the Maths exam, in the School Hall, same hours, Arithmetic and Algebra in the morning and Geometry and Calculus in the afternoon. What's Calculus? I don't know, I'm an English teacher. I got Higher Maths mind, but I don't think we did Calculus. Anyway, on Tuesday it's Spanish. Sorry, what? You don't do Spanish. I don't know, maybe you could learn some during the holidays – after all, Brian, you are going to Tenerife . . .'

I felt mildly bad, but no one was actually sobbing so I carried on, the exams and subjects becoming more numerous and abstruse.

In the class was a boy called Diamond. He was not a big boy, but he was wise before his time and very, very funny. In the first term, he was whacked by another boy during group work and I saw it.

'Findlay, why did you do that?'

'Diamond said I looked like a pig.'

'So,' says the jewel, 'Findlay hit me with his trotter.'

Anyway, seldom has the principle of Gestalt been more amply demonstrated than on that first of April when I was giving First Year their 'exam timetable'. Suddenly, the Diamond shouted, amid his despairing classmates, 'IT'S A LIE. IT'S AN APRIL FOOL. AAAAAAAAAARRRRRR-GGGHH'.

And threw his homework diary at me, followed by twenty-nine others.

I taught *Treasure Island* to that First Year class, and to many other First Year classes after them. I put them into competitive groups (these were different times) which I selected for a good academic and social balance and then I gave them quizzes and essays and marks for good answers (these were different times) and, from the beginning, told them they had to produce a 'project' twelve weeks later when we finished the novel. I should say that it always took me a very, very long time to deal with a text in class. I remember once an inspector saying that one of my colleagues had covered the whole first act of *Macbeth* in a double period. During exactly the same double period I had done the first scene of the same text, sixteen lines in all, some of them only one word ('Paddock' ... 'Anon' ... 'Macbeth'). Sometimes they read *Treasure Island* aloud (these were different times) and sometimes they staged scenes from it with actions (risk assessments not being required).

The projects based on the book could be anything. A lot of maps came in, variously steeped in tea or aged in the oven (one apologetic letter explained that a map so treated had been burned in its entirety). There were board games. Videos, often hysterically funny. Songs, to be performed by embarrassed boys. Once there was a glorious reconstruction of the captain's chest, perfect in every detail (where are you now, James?). And then there was Long John.

One dark December morning I entered my classroom early, switched on the light and screamed. At the back of the room, in the bay window, was a very tall man. On close inspection this proved to be an oversized model, about seven feet tall, of Long John Silver, constructed by a child called Martyn out of plywood, chicken wire and papier mâché, wearing an authentic coat sourced from somewhere, leaning on a crutch the boy had made, and – the *pièce de résistance* – with a parrot on his shoulder. Most extraordinarily for 1983, when you shook Long John's outstretched hand, the parrot said, 'Pieces of eight, pieces of eight!' A cassette, I think. This was a wonder indeed.

Fortuitously, an opportunity to display it publicly emerged on the school Open Day. The Head of English was very pleased with young Wyllie. Long John and a few other good pieces of *Treasure Island* arcana would form the department's display. I have to say, Long John was the star of the show, glowering away at the prospective pupils and their eager parents. Robin, the Principal, did his dutiful tour of the display, bringing his wife Fiona, who was always a gem, and his mother-in-law, who may, at some time, have been a gem, but was now ancient and grim.

'Hello, Cameron,' said Fiona. 'This is my mother.'

Mother did not seem overjoyed to meet me.

'And this is Long John Silver!' I said loudly to the old lady.

'I know that,' she responded, with the acidity which had, no doubt, won a war.

'And he talks, if you shake his hand.'

The old lady clearly thought I assumed she was senile, and made no move. Robin, irritated, grasped the hand and the parrot, set at its loudest, roared 'Pieces of eight!' in its other-worldly cackle. The old lady looked like she might pass out and Robin was very amused.

Thank you for making Long John, Martyn. Your 2021 Facebook page shows you with a nice woman and a child, and otherwise consists of photos of plates of sandwiches. This struck me as odd, but I hope you remember Long John and the day your creation nearly killed your Principal's mother-in-law.

Tripping: Dead Poets

In 1989, I was with a group of young people in Scituate, Massachusetts, as part of the Operation Friendship exchange programme. This was my fourth trip with OF and I was now a seasoned leader; in any case, this was a group that I knew very well and particularly liked, so I had no fears about them. Scituate is an old coastal settlement; its name derives from a Wampanoag word meaning 'cold brook' and is pronounced 'Sit-chuit'. With difficulty, I persuaded the group that pronouncing it 'Shit-you-ate' might be construed as disrespectful by our hosts, so by the time we arrived that joke was over.

I was hosted by one of the organisers, and since Operation Friendship was a church organisation in the States, I had the good fortune to be hosted by Alan and Rita Copithorne. Alan was the local minister, a very skinny, cheerful, moustachioed man who smoked heavily and liked doughnuts and coffee, and with whom I discussed many things but not religion. The programme of activities was an effortless success, including a baseball match in Boston. Baseball is a most peculiar game; indeed, it took me some time to realise that the game had begun, crammed as the action is into one tiny bit of the vast playing field. But I loved the atmosphere – the huge good-humoured crowd, the hot dogs and the Mexican waves. I had a very pleasant lady, one of our hosts, sitting next to me who was at least as uninterested in baseball as I was, and with whom I engaged in a lengthy discussion about tole-painting, which was her hobby. She was discussing the intricacies of applying paint to antique tin when there was a big roar and I looked at the pitch; the ball struck me square on the forehead and an obese man, previously peaceably sitting in front of me, threw himself on top of me, determined to get the ball, apparently a great prize. It was the first time an obese man had thrown himself on top of me for a decade; the previous occasion was at a party and involved an MP – I was twenty and he was not going after a baseball.

Anyway, it was a sunny and glorious time. Towards the end of the trip we spent an afternoon at the quayside, where there was an excellent ice cream shop (I am not interested in baseball, but I am fascinated by ice cream), and then a group of us proceeded to the nearby cinema. That party consisted almost exclusively of the boys from Stewart's Melville whom I had taught. The film was *Dead Poets Society*.

I was nine sessions into my career. When the school session started again a fortnight later, I was returning to a new job as a Housemaster; I was thirty-two and life was very good. Three of the boys with me that day were school debaters, and two of them had, the previous winter, become world champions. So we all sat there together in the incongruous darkness of a bright summer's day and watched the movie.

When we emerged blinking in the light, I could see that two of them were still in tears; I had myself been moved by the film but not excessively so – I liked Robin Williams a lot but so much of the story had felt fake to me, not least his character.

'My goodness, are you ok?' I said to one of them, a charismatic, very slightly deranged blond boy who was actually sobbing, and thus attracting some attention on the busy pier. It was like walking out of a film into another one.

'Well . . . yes . . .' he hyperventilated. 'It's just . . . he was just like you!'

'Christ, you don't all think that, do you?' I exclaimed in fear.

There was much nodding. Clearly, these boys who knew me very well thought I was like this self-important, two-dimensional, hysterical, rule-breaking, dangerous, unstable teacher. I could only think of all the reasons he would not gain recognition from the General Teaching Council for Scotland.

'But . . . but . . . I would never, ever, tear up a textbook – and that boy who killed himself – that was really the teacher's fault. It was right he was sacked. I mean they may have been really attached to him, but he wasn't good for them. And all the "Oh Captain! My Captain!" stuff, I mean, that was well over the top.'

They said nothing. They had two years left in school; I left Stewart's Melville with them to go to Heriot's, and was very moved to see these boys together crying on a low wall at the school on their last day. I had two years where periodically someone would shout 'Oh Captain! My Captain!' as I crossed the playground or entered a classroom. I was never very sure how I felt about this, but I tried not to dwell on it. I am not sure that too much self-scrutiny is good for the soul of the schoolteacher, or at least certainly this one.

I was very well established at Stewart's Melville when I left for Heriot's to take up my post as Head of English, and some kids felt betrayed by my departure. In particular I had a Second Year class that year, 1990-91, that I really loved. It did not please me to see them so sad and, maybe, bitter. One afternoon, I returned to my car and there was a bag of silver chocolate coins lying on top and a scrap of paper on which were the words 'count the coins'. Puzzled, I counted. Thirty pieces of silver.

Older Teacher

Stopping by Woods (and Killing Myself)

I went to university to study English so I could teach English, and had four glorious years during which I learned all sorts of things, a small proportion of them to do with English. One of the Monty Python team, I forget which one, said 'studying English at university is the next thing to studying nothing at all', which just about sums it up. We were meant to read lots and lots of stuff and actually read about thirty-five per cent of it, in preparation for tutorials which were often very jolly and lectures which were generally astonishingly precise in their subject matter and occasionally incapacitatingly dreary for those of us who actually turned up. These included three on 'Wordsworth and the Garden' which came with a four-page reading list; and several from an amiable Maltese gentleman on the Maltese presence in English Literature, which were illuminating but not helpful when, fifteen years later, I was readying myself to become Head of English at Heriot's.

Back at university, I specialised in US Literature and was taught by Faith and Nick: the latter trendy, clever and good-looking and the former a faintly eccentric, brilliant and cheerful woman whose age was anyone's guess, and who was intellectually twenty years ahead of her time. Faith had us reading Native American novels not even published in Britain, and, on hot afternoons in what was then called the David Hume Tower, talked about James Baldwin, who not only was black but, Lord above, also gay! Faith was very, very kind to me, and was even tolerant on the afternoon when it became clear that I did not know the rather crucial something that happened in Joseph Heller's *Something Happened*, which was that day's set text. When no one else seemed all that enthusiastic, she loudly supported me in becoming a teacher. After I had graduated I went back to see her, and accidentally walked in on her teaching, thinking she was alone. It was the next year's finals class and I was about to make my retreat. 'No, wait a minute,' she said. 'This is Cameron, who did this course last year. He's going to be a teacher. Isn't that marvellous!'

I was very touched, even if the wannabe publishers, journalists, 'writers' and, no doubt, merchant bankers sitting in front of her seemed less than impressed.

Still, my flatmate was a Law student, and read more novels than I did, while also becoming a qualified lawyer. I did not work as hard for my finals as I did for my Highers, but having, with difficulty, wrested the application form for teacher training from the Careers department of the university (they said, and I quote, I was 'too clever' to teach in a secondary school; looking back, I wonder if it was because I was too camp) I went off happily to Moray House, the best bit of which was the time actually spent in schools.

I really understood English Lit better by teaching it than by learning about it. There was so much I didn't like – when I arrived in teaching I wasn't keen on Shakespeare or much poetry. Even looking back on those twenty-five years or so when I taught a lot of English classes, I am aware that I only taught a limited range of things. Indeed, in my later years, when I wasn't teaching very much at all, I was always very keen to cover lessons in the English department, providing I could decide what I taught. Sometimes the class would be doing a text that I knew anyway, but mainly I returned to what one colleague called 'Cameron's Five Lessons'. This was a bit cheeky – I was the Principal, after all – but entirely accurate. Basically, after a while I only taught things I loved, and which I had taught for years.

There were exceptions. I came to Don Paterson's poetry very late on in my career, when I only had to teach half a Higher class a week. Don is a truly lovely man and he came to talk to us twice – once to the staff and once to the young people. He is a man who wears his intellect and learning very lightly, and whose poems are clever and moving. I was scared of them to begin with – teaching them, it was as if I had fallen off a horse years before and had to learn to ride again. But the class and I moseyed along with them and we all loved them.

One of the girls, when she was leaving, gave me the last lines of 'Nil Nil' inscribed on a picture of a road she had drawn, and I cried.

Mainly, though, I fell back into the old comfy armchairs of texts I had taught for decades. For the greater part of my career I only taught older students, and I taught them *A Streetcar Named Desire*, *Death of a Salesman*, Carol Ann Duffy (not *great*, but fab to teach), *Macbeth* (really the only Shakespeare I liked, but I loved it), *To Kill a Mockingbird*, 'Ode to Autumn' and Larkin.

I remember teaching a clever, difficult boy called Adam, grim but brilliant, witty, wonderfully cool, Larkin's 'Reasons for Attendance', that hard, personal poem written by a brilliant, difficult, not remotely cool man. In the poem, Larkin is looking in through the window of a jazz club and belittling those there; really he wants to be inside, chasing women and appreciating the music, but he pretends otherwise.

'What's this poem about, then?' I asked, having read it, trying to sound like Larkin, impersonal and clipped.

'The whole poem,' said young Adam, 'is an excuse.'

So clever, I wanted to bow to him.

And then there was Robert Frost. More or less a generation of Heriot's pupils had Frost's 'Stopping by Woods on a Snowy Evening' taught to them.

I love that poem and want it read at my funeral (should you be going, or even sending your apologies, or hosting a party, please remember that). I know it inside out, from the clever ambiguity of its opening line to the epiphany of its ending: '. . . miles to go before I sleep', which is repeated twice for reasons I took great delight in explaining to a shedload of pupils of various intelligences.

Towards the end of my career my partner and I visited the Robert Frost Farm in New Hampshire, where Frost wrote that poem. The tour was given by a young student, who was clearly greatly in love with Frost. 'This is the bed he slept in. This is the desk he sat at. This is the toilet he crapped in.' One of these he did not say, but he might have done. At the entrance to the farm there was, of course, a little shop, where I purchased a pretty illustrated version of 'Stopping by Woods . . .'

'You know this poem, sir?' the boy, now acting as shop assistant, enquired.

'I have taught it for years.'

There then followed a predictable conversation about where I taught, what the student was studying and how he came to work there. Then he said, smiling, 'You know, some people think this is a poem about suicide.'

'Of course it's a poem about suicide. I have taught it that way for thirty years. Frost says that he wants to lie down and die, then thinks better of it because he has responsibilities.'

I fear I may have then emitted a self-satisfied snicker.

Pause. Then this serious boy spoke again.

'I just think that's ridiculous.'

He was not for convincing. He knew a great deal about Frost. Jesus, he had met Frost's grandson. He had probably slept in that bed, sat at that desk and maybe even crapped ... In my dismay I thought it would have been a good conversation to have had thirty years earlier. It would have reminded me that just about every opinion out there counted – the poet's, the professor's, the twelve-year-old bravely putting her hand up. I will not be alone among teachers of literature in saying that my own understanding of many texts was enhanced or even radically informed by a child with their hand up.

But the Frost, that's about suicide, sonny.

Mother's Gin

Teachers spend a disproportionate amount of their time doing activities which by no definition could be classed as 'teaching'. Much has been made of their role as 'social workers' but social work is a skilled and respectable profession. I'm thinking more of their time spent as unqualified carers, supervising the business of growing up at the S1 disco, the S2 talent show, the S3 dance, the S4 ceilidh, the S5 ball, the S6 shagfest (one of these is not an actual thing, or at least that's not what it's called). I did lots of these supervisory tasks – single men and women, and younger staff, tend to do them more, not having the excuses of childcare or rheumatism to keep them from the fascina-tions of draughty school halls on wet nights near Christmas. If you're lucky you get to judge the 'best costume' competition, or do some French jiving with Ms Connor, or karaoke. My karaoke speciality was 'King of the Road', the arcane lyrics of which were a complete mystery to the youth of Edinburgh in 1995, but I always got a cheer for pluck.

I was crossing the playground one dark, dark night to take on the late shift of the S2 Christmas event, when I met two older boys who had also been roped in to help. They explained that one of the S2 boys had been caught red-handed with a cache of booze; with some admiration they reported that he had put away about half of a bottle of gin, or, at least, only half remained. He was, they said, 'pished'.

And so indeed it proved. He was standing just inside the door of the building, with Kenny Ogilvie, his kindly Year Teacher. Kenny's efforts to be stern were offset by his concern for the boy, who was a quite extraordinary shade of light green, later patented by Farrow and Ball in a shade called 'Eau de Puke'. Kenny had his hand on the boy's shoulder and was gently encouraging him to vomit into an enormous litter bin, which was usefully full of paper and lined with plastic.

'Come on, you'll feel so much better,' he said. 'Get it out of your system. Think of something disgusting,' he helpfully added. 'Think of a big greasy breakfast with three fried eggs covered in fat . . .'

At this point, the boy, who was, in fact, a very good boy, turned to express his thanks to Kenny with a piteous smile, and did indeed vomit copiously, missing the huge target of the bin entirely, but suc-ceeding in hitting Kenny's lovely suede shoes which, I fear, were never quite the same again.

Put off by the stink of ginny sick, I sped back outside, immediately bumping into the boy's mother, who had, of course, been summoned to remove this errant fruit of her loins. She was very, very angry.

'It's the kind of thing they do at that age – he'll never forget it,' I started, 'and he's a good boy usually . . .'

'That's very nice, Mr Wyllie,' she snarled. 'But it was my gin!'

Johnny Sleeps and Rory Dances

When the direction of my career shifted away from actual classroom teaching – which I loved and probably would have done for nothing – to senior management – which I liked and would not have done for less than 60k a year plus long holidays – the really big saving grace was meeting young people who wanted to get into Heriot's. They each got a forty-minute slot, and, with the assistance of my friend Jo, who was in charge of the admissions process administratively, I would sit and gently grill them about why (or if) they wanted to come. This led to many, many laughs, and a few discreet tears. One child, whom I went on to call Johnny B. Goode for the duration of his career at the school, was brought in aged eleven, late in the annual cycle, when a space had suddenly appeared in S1 for the following August. Johnny B's dad really wanted him to come to Heriot's, but it was clear that Johnny, polite though he was, really didn't, preferring to stick to plan and go to the local state school with his mates. I never really tholed this line of argument. Most boys make friends very easily, usually in large groups; years later, they go to some hellhole beach resort to drink cocktails from buckets and get burnt with exactly the same boys. They will then dance at each other's weddings and become serious, bald and sentimental.

Be that as it may, Johnny was having none of my blandishments and sat resolutely, answering my questions, kindly but monosyllabically. His dad, an amiable but determined man, got increasingly irritated with his first-born, and it was really hard for me to keep a straight face. Eventually I asked the tried and tested cliché of a question, 'What do you do in your spare time?' Now this question, given the skills and talents, real and imagined, of eleven-year-olds competing for a place, usually elicited a very impressive range of responses, focussing mainly on pre-Olympian feats of sport, an aspiration to be Jacqueline du Pré or Nelson Mandela or J. K. Rowling, or some footballer or rugby star of whom I, of course, had never heard. Johnny considered the question carefully and said, 'I like sleeping.'

His father looked homicidal. Jo and I laughed till we wept, and then

I said, 'Oh yeah. I love sleeping. It was a family hobby when I was a child. Other families went for long country walks after their Sunday roast. We had meatballs from a tin, a quarter of sweeties each, watched a film and fell asleep. I quite often just went to my bed in the middle of a hot summer's day and I still do.' All of which was true. Johnny and I were now fast friends, he came to Heriot's and did well, and his dad didn't kill him.

Anyway, I liked a competition, and in the highly competitive world of Edinburgh private education we reckoned ourselves a formidable admissions team. One of the highlights of the year was the day in June when all of the following year's First Year pupils came for induction. The kids progressing from our own Primary 7 were under strict instructions to be hospitable and kind to the new pupils. These came, in most years, from twenty-five or so different schools, many of them thus knowing nobody when they stepped through the gate on these sunny June mornings, with the Pipe Band practising on the lawns as they did for very, very, very long periods of time as the competitive piping season approached. Many of these young people, I later realised, believed that the band was playing for them.

The very last time I did this, while lunch was being eaten out of paper bags and the young people variously chatted or ran around and sometimes started friendships we knew would endure for decades – a girl saying hello to a girl at whose funeral she might speak seventy years later – we noted a boy standing away from the others, reading a book. He was a tall boy, conspicuously not talking, or chasing, or seeking out someone to do his eulogy. I knew who he was – a mild-mannered, clever fellow I had interviewed some months previously. While in general I had, of course, no problem with a child (particularly a boy) reading, I was a bit worried that he was lonely or shy and might not be having the necessary good time. So I set off towards him.

However, Rory had seen him too. Rory was an ebulliently cheerful, funny boy from our own Primary 7 who had clearly taken the message of welcoming others to heart, and as I watched he climbed up the edge of the banking and attempted to engage book-boy in conversation. The latter, only mildly distracted from his book, said only a few words, and Rory, disheartened, walked back down the bank, returning almost instantly with a pal. Again, however, book-boy stood, examined them briefly, and returned to his book. Rory's pal immediately retreated, feeling his duty was done, but Rory did not budge. And then, brilliantly, he began to dance. Really, truly, he ran down the banking, and turned and danced, and book-boy laughed. Here was a welcome indeed! And I laughed too, and then, very suddenly, it made me want to cry.

Angry

Being angry isn't very professional and I'm not really an angry person to begin with, but still ... I suppose I can look back and see five or six times in my career when I just lost it, though three of these were with the same member of staff. I actually once said to her, 'I think I need to remind you who you're talking to', then immediately felt bad, because of the pomposity, and the bad grammar. Then there was one boy, a very clever boy, who had been rude to a colleague and who came in to talk to Mr Dickson and me. He was pale and furious, and announced, five minutes into my patient ramble, that he had more important things to do than listen to me. I went berserk, and I think startled even Mr D, far less the child, who wept and wept, making me feel bad and good in equal measure.

Once, with a class I loved, a class I inherited when I arrived at Heriot's and taught for the three exam years, and most of them for their last year, a class which had been taught horribly in S1 and S2 and which would have welcomed anybody who didn't really hate them for being the clever, funny people they were, I got really angry.

I was teaching them *Macbeth* and I was really happy. I was reading the part of Macbeth, because I was the butchest person in the room (ok, they were fourteen, half of them were girls, and they were the top set) and they were so up for it. Then the phone rang. My beautiful wood-panelled room had a working fireplace, and was lined with books and was right at the top of a turret, meaning I kept fit and there was little chance of interruption. The little office at the back was badly neglected when I arrived – there was a hole at the bottom of one wall, through which one could actually see the quadrangle four floors below, and into which refuse had been thrown, presumably by generations of pupils. Anyway, the office was being fixed up, so the phone was in my classroom on my desk.

It rang and rang and rang. It stopped. Then rang and rang and rang again. Clearly, something was up, so I answered it, and the kindly receptionist said there was an angry parent on the line who would not give her name. The angry parent knew I was teaching, but would not call back. The class was by this time talking; I suggested they be quiet and read on, and I took the call.

A hysterical person began to shout at me; she would not give her name – indeed she would barely stop shouting. Her anger was, fortunately, not aimed directly at me, but at one of the other English staff whom, she asserted, had slighted her daughter's work in a way which upset said daughter. I attempted to calm her, while at the same time stopping to tell the class to read, not to talk. Actually, most of them were gaping at me – I'm sure they could hear the ranting disembodied voice at the other end of the phone.

There were two fabulous girls in this class who were friends and sat together; one was outgoing, creative and very lovely; the other had a crystalline intelligence, was generally shy and very lovely. They were talking and giggling.

'Girls! Please be quiet!' I demanded.

'I will not be quiet!' shouted the woman on the phone. 'I think I will consult my lawyer,' then she hyperventilated enough for me to say, 'I really need to call you back.'

'I'm not telling you who I am!' she screamed. 'If I do it'll just be taken out on Pollyanna.' (Not her daughter's real name.) Now I knew who she was, at least.

'I promise nothing will be said to Pollyanna,' I whispered in the interests of confidentiality, clearly failing. The girls turned to each other. They knew who this was. The gossip was out. Bugger.

'Penguin! Slamdunk!' I shouted (not their real names). 'Be quiet!'

The class was amused. I was not.

'I will not be quiet!' said Pollyanna's mother, yet more hysterically.

'I'm sorry,' I said. 'I wasn't talking to you. I am teaching.' (This was a lie. I was pacifying a hysterical person to the amusement of some young people.) 'I will call you back as soon as I can. Goodbye.'

I hung up. I was furious, and this wasn't helped by a smattering of applause.

'You two! Penguin! Slamdunk! I thought girls were supposed to be more responsible! You two are a disgrace to your gender!'

I was really angry, and the class fell silent. These two girls, whom I adored, looked stricken, which, at that moment, pleased me.

Pins dropped. Then a brilliant boy, who was about three-foot-two at the time (I danced at his wedding) took a big risk.

'Mr Wyllie?'

'Yes, what, Paul?' His real name.

'Do you know you're lovely when you're angry?'

Christmas

By Christmas, everyone in a school is exhausted. The term has been long, the weather often bleak, and Christmas itself is a huge production, particularly for primary school teachers – though, mind you, they do get shedloads of presents to wheelbarrow out to their cars, or at least they did, until someone decided that it might lead to favouritism. (As an aside – I might have favoured a child more for the gift of a Caribbean cruise, but not for a mug that says 'I thrive on stress' – though I do like that one anyway, in case she's reading.) There's nativities and concerts and plays and outings to the panto; there's church services and staff parties and presents for the janitors, if one has any sense; there's speeches to write and scripts to learn and, for the latter chunk of my career at Heriot's, there was the Christmas Event.

The Christmas Event was my fault. Given that ninety per cent of Scottish kids never go anywhere near a church, I suggested that maybe every second year we could have a secular event rather than a religious one. This was a terrible mistake – going next door to the church and singing carols was so EASY and gave most of the kids an opportunity to rest, whereas the Christmas event had to be ORGANISED. And really, by the time you get to it, the young people are exhausted too, from exams and parties and sport and drink and the pursuit of love. To be honest, there probably isn't much that would entirely engage their attention on a school stage that didn't involve food or money being thrown at them by a selection of celebrities in a state of undress. Still, they were kind young people, so we got by.

In order to apologise to Ailsa, whose job it was to organise this thing, I always gave an address of some sort. It filled in a slot. I tried to be amusing and thoughtful, but by the time I came to write it, usually the day before, I was so tired I could hardly see. Obviously, there were moments leading up to Christmas of great joy, usually occasioned by the Nursery Nativity (a fairly insane event which left parents delirious with glee, as some child – a sheep, a tree or the Mother of God yelled out, 'Hello Granny, hellloooo Graaaannny', causing Granny, full of love and wonder, to shout back) or by the Junior School Nativity, a very, very different affair, with production values worthy of Cameron Mackintosh, actual choreography and lovely costumes. I will not readily forget the Three Wise Men from P2 – one sweet child, one dilly and one sportsman, the last clearly in charge. The dilly forgot his gift, and stared blankly into the lights at the front of the stage until the squat sporty boy, clearly destined for great leadership roles in the future, shouted 'Get your gift!' at him, thrusting his own myrrh at the poor child as an example.

However, one year at the Christmas Event I gave this talk:

When I was younger, I used to get very excited about Christmas; when I say younger, I don't mean when I was eight or ten – I mean up until I was about twenty-seven. I wasn't brought up in a religious family, and I wasn't even brought up in a very sentimental family. I used to get excited – often to the point I felt bilious – at the prospect of eating, drinking and the endless possibilities of new stuff. Our house was filled with Christmas decorations of the most kitsch variety, including a remarkably noisy disembodied Santa head, which was put on the outside door and which blared 'Merry Christmas!' every time anyone came close to it, and of which I was particularly afraid.

Between the ages of zero and about ten, Christmas followed the same pattern every year. We would get up at about four o'clock in the morning to open the presents. My mother liked sleeping and was often in a mood that varied between pretending to be jolly and actually sleeping. My father, the life and soul, would have set everything up beautifully to make sure we got exactly what we wanted, our Christmas lists being carefully edited earlier to fit a generous but not unlimited budget. My brother and I would then play with whatever we'd got, my father would cook and eat breakfast, and my mother would sleep, so we were all, in essence, doing what we liked best.

Later we would watch Laurel and Hardy on the telly, then get dressed and go to my grandparent's house; my mother's parents lived in Stirling and gave us Christmas lunch and my dad's parents would come there too. On the long drive to Stirling – this being before the M9 was even thought of – we would play a game where we watched out for kids on new bikes, out riding them on Christmas morning, and we used to see a hundred of them on the road to Stirling every year. There we would sit down to Christmas lunch, being served in the order that Jenny, my mother's mother, liked us – or at least that was how our family interpreted it. Certainly I always came several people after my tall blond brother, but edged in before either my dad or my grandfather, her husband, so I thought I did pretty well.

There was, of course, Christmas pudding, made by my incredibly aged spinster Auntie Meg, and full of silver threepenny bits which were dutifully collected, once from the back of my throat, at the end of the meal, to be recycled for the next year. But the highlight of the meal for me was the trifle. It was the finest trifle ever known to man, and I am very, very, very keen on good trifle. It came from Stirling Home Bakeries, now sadly closed down, and was a massive thing, enough for twenty or twenty-five. At the end of the day, when our second set of presents had been duly packed in the car, my gran would give my mother the trifle to take home. One Boxing Day morning, when I was about eight, I got up and ate a great chunk of that glorious trifle; my father took the blame, for which I only loved him more.

After we'd had our lunch, Santa would arrive. He would appear outside my gran's sitting-room window, and tap on the glass. Being a child of nervous disposition, I was always terrified. Then he would come in and distribute the presents. I continued to be terrified. Santa was, in this instance, my grandfather, Papa Joe, a retired coalminer who had fought in the Great War and been in the General Strike. One year I caused great hilarity, as Santa went out the door to his sleigh – which was, by necessity, parked some distance away – by commenting that Santa was wearing Papa Joe's slippers. Being a kindly soul, I always thought it sad that Papa Joe missed Santa's visits and told him so.

I have been thinking a lot about this very recently, because on Saturday I transferred my gran, Jenny, now 96, into an old folks' home, and I did so with great relief. Her life, of late, has not been so filled with family or friends; her eyes have gone, she doesn't eat well and so on – but she still talks with great happiness about these Christmases, fifty years ago. While the central theme of today's event is the child, and so I have told you about my childhood, we should spare a thought too for all the old folk at Christmas time. There is a song by the American singer John Prine which says that while trees, as they age, grow stronger, and old rivers flow more quickly, lonely old people wait for someone to say, 'Hello in there, hello.'

Many of you will have elderly neighbours, elderly relatives or elderly people you sit next to on the bus. They may be lonely at Christmas. It would be good of you to say 'hello in there' to them.

I hope you all have a truly wonderful Christmas. Thank you.

Now, I was really pleased with that, and thus with myself. There was, as customary, a mild but appreciative bit of applause and a lot of smiley faces, which I allowed myself to think were to do with the amusing but thoughtful content of my speech, rather than the blindingly obvious reason that that was the end of the event and the kids were then released for two glorious weeks.

This was all short-lived. I stepped outside into a chilly but sunny playground and started saying 'Have a lovely Christmas!' to anyone who passed, mostly fleeing towards fun.

And then Dominic came up. He stood in front of me, smiled very sympathetically as if at an object of pity and said, 'Hello in there.'

Gabriel on a Train

If I had been offered my first job in a state school I would have taken it, and I don't know if I ever would have moved to an independent school. You can move that way – private schools are often very welcoming to state school teachers, who sometimes wrongly think life will be easier when they make that move. It isn't any easier, it's just different. You can't, however, usually move the other way, from a private school to a state school, at least not to any kind of promotion; you are tarnished, spoiled, unclean. You have not served.

Anyway, fate took me to DSMC and on to Heriot's. I didn't really think about the politics of it much, though I could understand why, in Edinburgh, with its vast array of independents, teachers in state schools could be scathing about the private sector. There's this notion about 'real life', as if a kid from a housing estate is 'realer' than a kid at a fee-paying school. All are real to me, individuals, with individual needs to be catered for, academically and pastorally. But there was, of course, a ton of prejudice on both sides. Private school kids were seen as a) arrogant, b) narrow-minded, c) conceited, d) having a sense of entitlement, e) privileged, f) snobs, g) rich, h) homosexuals, i) homophobes, j) racist, k) having posh voices, l) Tories who lived in big houses, with servants, m) only getting into good universities because their headmaster had slept with someone important in the university when they, too, were in private schools, o) having small dicks (the boys), p) hating the poor, q) having names like Tarquin Cholmondley-Featherstonehaugh, r) not caring what was going on

70

in the 'real' world, s) being dead soft when kicked in, t) taking fancy drugs, u) wearing pink-striped hats in the summer, v) not having real friends, w) shooting poachers on their land, x) well, well, I've got to x without even thinking about it. Statistical analysis by a team of international experts finds that the above list is only twenty-seven per cent accurate.

Meanwhile, their counterparts in state schools were 'chavs'.

I *hated* that word. I don't really know what it means. However, I accept that the co-existence of two sectors of education, public and private, inevitably creates prejudice. Snobs and chavs. Simple as that. Fight, fight, fight, I say. Hold fast to what is right, I say. Respect each other as co-combatants in the great war against adults!

Thomas and Gabriel and I are on a train. It is Saturday and we have been in Aberdeen for a debating competition. They are wearing school uniform, and they have special coloured pockets on their blue blazers which say 'DEBATING' in inch-high white embroidered capital letters. They have won, praise be, and on our table on the train home we have a big, big trophy. Down at the other end of the carriage is my friend Mick and the team from Stewart's Melville.

I like Thomas and Gabriel. Thomas is an easy-going, constantly smiling, very clever boy; a boy of sound moral character, some wit and much kindness, who looks a bit like a very amiable fox. He is easy to work with, conscientious and punctual; he is, I am sure, going to be a lawyer, have three children, and live a wholly decent life. I like and admire him for all these things.

Gabriel. Ah, Gabriel. Brilliant, bohemian, amazing-looking. Went through his naughty period when he was ... what, fourteen? Stylish, elegant, very funny but introspective, inclined to gloominess. Always late, always really sorry. Loyal, thoughtful, modest, unexpected. And the only person called Gabriel I ever taught. He was going to be either very rich or very poor, but I think, if I was eighty and I asked him nicely, he would gladly give me a tenner, whether millionaire or pauper.

So we are content in each other's company on that train, with no intention of much talking. Gabriel reads a novel, Thomas *The Times* and I prepare to fall asleep. I was up at 6 am and it is just before

5 pm, and I look forward to my late dinner back in Edinburgh and, in particular, some alcohol. These competitions are a curious mix of brief excitements and lengthy lacunae, only made tolerable by the presence of lots of people, teachers and pupils, whom you know. This is the life of people who enjoy niche activities: the constant round of competitions, practices, camps, fundraising, qualification for the next level. Think the Pipe Band (committed parents, great cakes), horse-riding (expensive, healthy, good for posture, requires a horse), basketball (tall, intense, sportsmanlike, squeaky); it doesn't matter what it is – it's as much about friendship as about what actually happens. Hint: avoid swimming at all costs – very early mornings, bad hair, bad skin, damp and too competitive.

At 4.59 pm, just as the whistle blows, a large group of young men get on the train. One sits beside me, facing the boys, completing our four. Four more sit on the opposite side of the aisle, four more behind us, four more in front. Thirteen young men, and they are, if not actually pissed, a bit drunk. The train lurches out of Aberdeen, and these guys are making a great deal of noise. All I want to know is where they are getting off, because then I can sleep. But all the man next to me wants to know is what the trophy's for, so he asks Thomas, who blushes deeply, and looks at me.

'Thomas, speak to the guy!' I say. Thomas beams, still purple, and, unusually tentative, says 'Debating'. Gabriel is furious, tight-lipped, stressed by all this noise. The man next to me – maybe twenty-two – is immune to all these signs and will not simply talk to his many friends.

'Debating? What have you been debating?' he says.

'They've been in a competition in Aberdeen,' I say, then add, redundantly, 'they won.'

'So what were you . . . debating about?'

The three of us are aware that some of his gang are now interested.

'Tell the guys what you've been debating about . . .'

So Thomas begins, with a discourse about something they talked about that day. Freedom of the press? The EU? Gender? Prisons? Drugs? I can't remember, but as soon as he begins, all thirteen of these guys – who are, I have by this time ascertained, from Peterhead and will be getting off in two stops – begin to discuss it too. Thomas relaxes, and soon he and these young men, some of them no older than him, are more or less having a debate, shouty and fuelled by cans, which we are all offered; I refuse on the boys' behalf. Gabriel is still focused firmly on his book, when the chief guy – he seems older and in charge – says directly to him, about some arcane point, 'What do you think?'

Gabriel says nothing.

'He's a bit shy,' I say, which is sort of true, 'but he's a great debater. He's going to represent Scotland in the summer.'

Gabriel, an old friend, looks like he wants to chop me into small pieces.

'For fuck's sake, son,' the guy says, 'that's fantastic. This guy – what's his name?'

'Gabriel,' I say, for that is his name.

'Gabriel ... he's representing Scotland at debating? That is fantastic, man. Here, Fraser, did you hear that? We were celebrating in Aberdeen today because Fraser's got into uni – he's going to Abertay. Fraser, this guy's representing Scotland at debating!'

Fraser, cheerful, very young, shy, appears from behind, and sticks his hand out to Gabriel, and Gabriel, abashed, shakes it. I am, unexpectedly, terribly moved. I didn't know that Fraser had got into uni. I just thought they were drunk. I didn't think these men would really be interested in debating. I didn't know they wouldn't laugh when they found out Gabriel's name was Gabriel. They are my father sixty years earlier, that's all.

For the remaining little while, there is a good-natured rammy of argument. Peterhead moves into view just as they ask about abortion, and I stop that, because abortion is the one thing school debaters are never asked to debate about.

There is much hand-shaking. Much wishing of good luck for Gabriel in the World Championships. I think they will remember meeting a boy called Gabriel who is representing Scotland. As they move down the train, they come upon the Stewart's Melville boys in their bright red blazers, and they chant 'You won fuckin' nothin'! You won fuckin' nothin' . . .' at them, much to our amusement. At school, on Monday, I talk at Assembly about how much I hate the word 'chav'.

Where is Tes?

This is about two people really, about Sam and Tes, and it is not a laugh at all.

My working life was, for all of its thirty-seven years and five months, a joy. When I started teaching I hated the summer holidays – I spent all my money on cheap trips, beer and cakes, then hung around in Edinburgh waiting for term to start so I could meet new kids, and stand in a classroom and teach them. I know I have been shielded from the sadness and triumph of working with really disadvantaged children, and very occasionally I wonder if I would have succeeded if I had done that, or whether it would have ground me down and ironed me out. I worked plenty hard, but really each happy school year melded into another on a tide of goodwill, as each wave of bright-eyed, funny, mainly clever, often hard-working boys and girls went off into their lives. Mostly, they were 'sorted', they knew where they were going, they could go there; there was little, in truth, to stop them.

Some other people's lives are not so easy, and I am not inured against their stories.

In 1996, Sam Mort came to work in the English department at Heriot's. She was a striking-looking girl from Kingussie, clever, mischievous and a modern woman, by which I mean that she said what she thought to both men and women. Consequently, some people didn't like her much, but those who did adored her, both teachers and students. She was a brilliant teacher, full of humour, often outrageous, obstinate, creative and she lit up the room, sometimes by shining a searchlight and sometimes by setting it on fire. I think I might have been a little scared of her at first, although I was, by that time, fairly senior; but then I became an acolyte and loved her.

She stayed five years and when she left she did not go on to a promoted post in another school or a secondment to some educational quango. Instead she went to do VSO (Voluntary Service Overseas), training teachers and herself teaching in Eritrea. On the second day there she rejected accommodation in the sweltering concrete building that her lofty position accorded her, and asked to sleep in a mud hut. At night she would see the boys and girls from the little town gathering to study under the one street lamp, desperate to learn.

Time passed, and two years later she left Eritrea to work in a palace in the Middle East. But that is another story, which she can eventually write herself in a book to be called *From a Mud Hut to a Palace*. I cannot imagine whom they will cast as her in the film, but I hope Brad Pitt will consider playing me, even if it entails losing a lot of weight.

When she left Eritrea, Sam left behind a number of students who adored her and whom she loved, and one of them was a boy called Tesfagherghish Weldeghebreil. She asked if the school could sponsor him and, because it was her, of course we did. I told the school about him at Assembly, and lots of the kids gave a pound each and we started to send the money to Eritrea to support Tes, as we called him, just as, in *Great Expectations*, Philip Pirrip was called Pip. Never very much; I think £30 a month was enough and, as we came to know Tes better from his exuberant, idiosyncratic, joyful letters, there was plenty 'Tes money' to give to others too.

Scottish schools do this kind of thing. They sponsor schools in other countries, sometimes for a very long time. Their students go to visit and to help, to build toilet blocks in Malawi and decorate orphanages in Kenya. We wanted Tes to succeed and to thrive, and to maybe even be the doctor he dreamt of being.

Our young people loved his letters. He called me 'Mr Cameron' and said I was his father and his brother. On cold winter mornings in Edinburgh, our young people laughed at the concept of my fathering a six-foot athletic black man, and then they settled to listen to his astonishing prose. This is part of the first letter he wrote in February 2003:

My parent live in Beleza and I live with my uncle in Agordat my parent (my father and mother) old they can'n work well my father salaries is 300 nakfa (8 pound) in a month. This is not enough for us because there are many (8) babies. So I am learn and as well as work in deeging in order help my families. This is very hard to me. It is opposite to my education but never had being stop (absent) in my class. I am also a cyclining I was very race in cycling copitition I came chapion in my region in 2001-2002 but now I am stoped because my cyckle is damage and it is not modern it coust 800 nakfa (15 pound) so I do not have money to check it so I am still stoped in cycling.

Then:

I have 3 brothers older than me. One of them was when he dies 8th Grade by some accident he dead. After he deeded my oldest brother he finished high school and he done test (national examination) but at that time monst of the student got bad russal so he field at 11th Grade. So he left in Sawa (military place).

You know, these Heriot's kids really cared about this boy. They came in droves to look at photos of him – very tall, smiling, getting his school prizes. And, as time passed, it became clearer and clearer that he was really clever. I have his actual school report for 9th Grade, signed very faintly by his sick father. In the first term Tes was first out of fifty-five, in the second first out of forty-three, in the third first out of thirty-seven. Other kids left for Sawa to join the military, where Tes did not want to go. Mr Teame Araia, his teacher, added: 'Not only he stood first out of his class, he is one of the outstanding students in the school; and if he continues in this way, he will succeed. He has a bright future.'

But to have a bright future in Eritrea is not easy, indeed barely possible, and Tes knew that. Still, for the next two years his letters were full of chat and humour, with each one thanking us and God, though every time, amid the positive love, there came the name Sawa again and again.

In February 2005:

In the time we take examination. Inspite of bing difficul the test
I score very good mark. As a result in the 1st semester of 2004/05
I am gating the 1st rank in my school from grade 11. I am looking
forward know [he had scored out 'liking' and put in 'looking'],
I was completed my high school. But some thing happen to me.
There is no chance to continuous my school becous there is big-
gest problem of Sawa (militar camp) may have more chance to
become soldier but I don't want to become a soldier. Mr Cameron
Wylli I am always going to remmber your kindness up on me as
well as George Heriot School. I am never forgate you until I am
die. When I write this paper I was carying a tear drop from my
eye. I fell abnormall just give me your hand I need know support
from you. I need a candle to escape from darkness.

And then silence. Sam feared he was doing what so many young
Eritrean students had tried to do before, which was to escape going to
Sawa military academy, along with 15,000 other boys and girls each
year. Once there they faced what Human Rights Watch calls 'indefinite
national service', preparing them to play a part in the border conflict
with Ethiopia which went on for twenty years from 1998. There were,
in theory, schools at Sawa, but the teachers were themselves young
conscripts; students who survived said they learnt nothing and were
enslaved as workers in a dusty hellhole at 42 degrees centigrade.

So students would flee conscription and so did Tes. Two months
later, he emailed Sam from Khartoum:

About my journye yes you are correct it is so dangoroys. I started
from befare a manth when I left my school at that moment I
felt bodly but I continuous my journey to the broader of Eritrea,
Ethiapa and Sudan. Is boarder is very dangours. Befare naw
many people are die & many people also captured by the solieder
of Eritrea up to now they are in a presin. Yes it is more luck! to
reach here.

He was, in fact, captured by Sudanese soldiers who sent him to prison for a week, and then moved on to a UNHCR camp. Then, by some process we don't know, he arrived in Khartoum, got a job as a waiter, and by good luck found someone else from Agordat who looked after him.

So, I am sitting in Corstorphine in my dad's house and I am giving him an update about Tes. He was a good and kind man, George Wyllie, and he valued education and hard work; he would have paid for Tes himself if I let him, and probably given him a room in a bungalow in Corstorphine. I am telling him that Tes is in Khartoum and seems, for the moment, reasonably safe. Then my stepmother, whose conversation often tended towards herself and her friends, said, 'Khartoum? That's where Tony and Marne are going. On Tuesday.'

It seemed unlikely to me that my stepmother had friends who were imminently going to Khartoum, and I wondered if she had misheard, mistaking Khartoum for, say, Kirkintilloch. But – ye of little faith – my father nodded; this was right. These people of whom I had never heard were indeed going to Khartoum on Tuesday. So I got in touch with them, these kind, good people, who were bound there I think on church business, and they, astonishingly, arranged to meet Tesfagherghish. On 14 May 2005, they sat at a café in Khartoum and spoke to this boy, this leading character in the collective psyche of our school, this real person, and three days later they sent me an email:

> Tes tells us he wants to enter a school here that does its teaching in English, so that he can get on with his education. Tes is a little unsure exactly what direction to go in, but he seems to lean towards the sciences and is very good at Physics. So that would seem a good choice career-wise because it can go in all sorts of directions. Anyway, we can try to help him as much as we are able. He's certainly very motivated. He starts school in June so we will have to move fast to confirm a place. Where do we go from here?

Well, at Heriot's, the senior pupils had wristbands made and sold 250 at £2 each for his school fees. One of the staff had a friend who worked in a school in Khartoum and she was approached. Sam contacted someone else she knew. I approached two schools and explained the situation ...

But on the same day that Tes had met Tony and Marne, I had an email from him. Half of it was very excited about finding a school and going to it in Sudan, but the other half showed he was still desperate to get to Europe, poor boy:

> I had bad idea to go to Italiy this is because I want to continou my school & sport there I have a big dream after same year I hope I could reach it. I think so many things I will become but the way that I choice is very dangerouse, yes I remember so many Eritrea were back to Eritrea no one knows where they are.

However, by the end of that month things were looking a lot sunnier and more stable. Tes had found a school to start in late June and a house to share – $80 a month – he apologised for the cost. Still, only a fortnight later he told Sam he had decided to try to cross the Sahara to get to Libya, and from there on to Italy – she and I tried to stop him.

> Yes Sam I know this is so dangerouse way. So many people were die & still Die. But I have dicided it to go there Sam I know you feel so bad about this because you have seen life is so expensive If once go never turn back. But if I stay here also I am sure it is the worst (dangoures) because I have see what happen to here for Eritrean people myself you Mr cameron are good think for me still. Also for future if I alive I believe you.

Both of us tried to tell him not to do this but he disappeared, and then a fortnight later:

> Hello. . .mr camero. how are you? Mr Cameron I am so sorry for what I have done. I am save I am not sure what is the name of the place I am living in now I think it is Benkaziz 500 millies from

Tripoly Capital city of lbya mr I was in the rural of the sahra desert far about 14 days. it is so dangerouse no water no food no living things except sand soil. Mr cameron & sam you are save my life in Eritrea sudan even if in Tripoli lbya thanks more I will never forgiet you

Loss but never forgeitness yourse brather student tes

'Loss but never forgeitness.' I wish I had known how true that was.

And then, for a while, there was silence and Sam and I thought he had died. Having told the school Assembly the story of Tes getting to Benghazi, there was nothing to tell them for a long time. The kids, the younger ones particularly, who had worn the wristbands with such joy, would stop me and say 'Where is Tes?' But, for a while, there was no answer.

Then nearly a year later, a final email. He had been in prison in Tripoli for nine months:

I saffer sick [ill] becouswe of the condition of prison is not good concentration of people lead to transfer to this deases [sickness] generally prison in Libya is very bad . . . I can't fargate from my brean so when I will ok, you, Sam & me will decise. Mr Cameron as you are my father & my teacher we 3 of as will do what I do once in Libya then may be my life will go to the right way but now I look for my health because my body is very very week. So Thanks for looking after me with out tired thanks more.

And then nothing else. There were no contact details to follow. I decided not to share this last email with the school because it was laden with doom, even when, a few weeks later, it was the end of term, and the Sixth Year, about to leave into the summer suns and live their lives, asked me 'Where is Tes?' It was a year since I had said anything about him. For a long time, I thought he might just turn up – Sam told me that another of her former pupils had just, one day, appeared in Cardiff. But no, that was not to be, and I cannot now think he is alive.

Beside me here is a beaded bracelet he sent me. The letters picked out on it are CWHMGHS (Cameron Wyllie Head Master George Heriot's School). Here is the end of the second letter he wrote to me, in 2003, this boy who, three years later – starved, imprisoned, ill, just disappeared; probably not even a statistic anywhere, but very, very real to me and a thousand young Scots:

> My school is nearly open for 2003–2004. I am now in gread 10th. I am very happy to start and stay in school and also my family was said thanks for all thanks for halp me. I promise you I will study hard because education is sunlight.

Tripping: The Art of Drinking

I went on many school trips, but the ones I liked best were with the Art department. I was allowed on these trips in part because I liked Art, but mainly because I was male, and they needed a man to look after the – let's be honest – fairly small number of boys who went on Art trips. I loved the students who studied Art and I also loved their teachers, clever people who worried about what they wore and made their own jewellery and who had skills which I wholly lacked; skills which they demonstrated as they sat and sketched in Paris or New York. Of course, they also loved shopping, and I love shopping too, particularly when surrounded by cheerful young people with taste.

In Uniqlo on Fifth Avenue, in theory supervising some Art students, I tried on a hat and Struan, a boy of immense coolness who knew how to dress, said, 'Great hat. Buy it.' So I bought it for $8 in the sale. Even now, if I go out in my recently purchased artfully curated jacket and trousers, wearing the carefully selected shirt, and the discreet but effective overcoat, and the stylish but understated shoes, total strangers will say 'Great hat'. Some people might find it humiliating that a child has much more taste and style than they do, but I gave in years ago. Artists have chosen my clothes, my spectacles, even the colours of the paint in my house, and I am happy to let them.

One of our trips was to Barcelona. It was a peculiarly cheap trip, possibly because of the mode of travel, which saw us fly from Edinburgh to Heathrow, then take a coach all the way to Spain. The young people didn't seem to mind, and all that long way were hugely amiable, although there was one rather needy girl whose mother had clung to her at the airport; she did not endear herself to me in the middle of the night on a motorway in France when she woke me from my troubled sleep to tell me she had lost a shoe. She was a clever girl, but like so many she found it difficult when the umbilical cord was once again cut. Still, I have no idea what she wanted me to do about her shoe.

Our trip was going very well. Catriona and Amanda and I were very happy with these grand Art students – biddable, amusing, charming, talented. And then we went to the jousting.

Jousting? Medieval jousting? Well … the difficulty with school trips is what you do in the evenings once you have eaten. The eating on such trips is usually fairly rudimentary and somewhat rushed. In Chinatown in NYC, we had a meal at 6.30 pm one October night; the food was spectacular, but our enjoyment was somewhat diminished because the staff of the restaurant had their coats on ready to leave after about twenty minutes. Generally young people eat so fast, or not at all, which is worse, just at the point when it would be good for them to linger over dinner so that time passes and they can reasonably be expected to go to bed when you return to the hotel. This is not easy if it's only 7.32 pm.

So you go bowling, or to the cinema. Or you succumb to the whim of the travel company and go to watch medieval jousting. Dinner was included. It was quite cheap and involved a bit of a journey there and back. Do it, then beddy-byes. Sweet.

Actually, the journey there was much longer than anticipated because our coach driver, who swore he knew exactly where we were going, didn't know where we were going. I do know a bit of Spanish, but stopping the coach and asking random passers-by required me knowing the Spanish word for 'jousting'. That wasn't happening, but eventually we more or less chanced on the place. It was an enormous open-air stadium, and we were hurried in because the service of dinner, which preceded the show, had begun. It was very dark inside and our party was broken up; the kids disappeared into the musty gloom, and the three staff were seated together. As our eyes adjusted, we could see the young artists spread around the vast space in tight little groups, among a crowd of maybe a thousand people, all, of course, tourists. In front of each of us was a place-setting, a glass and . . . a bottle of wine.

In the darkness a disaster loomed. Where was the manager? I set out to find him and asked in terrible Spanish: please tell the staff that the wine is to be taken away from the young people. Of course, *Senor*. It was impossible for my lady colleagues and I to do anything, for the show was beginning, the light dimmed in the eating areas and searchlights exploded in the centre of the stadium. A great cheer arose as some buggers in helmets and armour rode into the ring.

We ate the terrible food and tried to watch the jousting, which had all the authenticity of a WWF wrestling match. The wine was horrific so we didn't drink it on principle. Occasionally the lights would flicker across the crowded benches of the stadium and we might pick out one of our own, smiling happily at this display of Spanish culture. At least we hoped it was that. These were good kids, we said. They know that they will get in trouble if they drink, we said. The Head Teacher is with us, Catriona, who had organised the trip, said. I personally was less convinced by this final argument.

And then the interval. Using the lateness of the hour as an excuse (it was 8.35 pm) we scurried about trying to find the young people to send them back to the bus. Even in normal circumstances this is roughly like herding mongeese; on that night in the crowded half-light it took ages, but eventually, we counted them all back out again. When I got to the bus, they were standing around outside, horribly cheerful. The driver asked for a word.

'Some of them ur pished,' he commenced. 'Now, if thur sick on the bus, I will no' be happy. Fuckin' ridiculous.'

I relayed this information, more or less word-perfectly, to my lady colleagues. Catriona, who is a loving, warm, happy, positive, caring person by nature, was absolutely furious, tight-lipped, pale. The kids looked visibly less happy, some whitening, some . . . a bit green. We knew this was a long journey.

'YOU HAVE SPOILT THIS TRIP FOR EVERYONE. YOU KNOW YOU ARE NOT ALLOWED TO CONSUME ALCOHOL ON SCHOOL TRIPS!' she yelled. 'MR WYLLIE WILL DECIDE WHAT IS GOING TO HAPPEN TO THOSE OF YOU WHO HAVE BEEN DRINKING.' Then as an after-thought, 'WHO HAS BEEN DRINKING?'

'Any amount at all?' asked one fool, perhaps having tasted the rotgut and rejected it. In his case, he probably asked for the wine list.

'ANYTHING AT ALL!' Catriona screamed.

About half of them shakily put their hands up.

'Right, over here,' I said, leaving the ladies to look deeply into the eyes of the innocent. Amanda, the Head of Art, looked so sad and saint-like it was impossible that any child could sustain a lie.

However, once I had moved the drinkers sufficiently far away, I began with the obvious and necessary question – was there anyone over there who should be over here? Honour among thieves and all that. But really, it seemed likely that the forces of teenage morality had split along the lines I would expect.

'Now,' I said. 'Mrs Fraser is furious with you. You have let us all down. In theory I should be considering whether to send you home [we had about twenty hours left in the country]. But . . . to be honest, my major worry is the journey back to the hotel. The driver knows you have been drinking. He thinks this is my fault. He thinks you are a bunch of spoiled and entitled privately educated brats who will vomit all over his bus. A great deal of what I will do at the hotel depends on that not happening. "The quality of mercy is not strained."'

I paused, considering that I might punish them by explaining what that much misunderstood line actually means. But instead I pressed on with brief individual chats, and it seemed to me that only one or two of them were really drunk.

One of these was a lovely boy called Oliver, a really talented artist, cheerful and clever and probably, truth to tell, actually a bit spoiled. Drink was, I fear, not unknown to Oliver. He wasn't very, very drunk, but a bit pale and sorry for himself. The other main offender was Miss Needy of the missing shoe, who kept assuring me loudly she was fine. I suggested that if she said she was fine once more, it seemed very likely Mrs Fraser would throw her off the bus and leave her on the motorway.

We boarded the bus. Oliver, on my instructions, sat by himself on the front seat beside the door. I sat opposite him, behind the driver, to observe. The lady art teachers sat behind me, enraged. The driver kept the door open and got going. I attempted to engage Oliver in conversation in order to keep his mind off vomiting, but eventually, politely, he closed his eyes and pretended to slumber. My fingers were very crossed. Everything looked promising. Catriona even laughed at something I said. The bus roared on, the driver simmering.

It was then that Miss Needy made her move. Unannounced, she shambled up to the front of the bus and sat down beside Oliver.

'Miss Needy,' I said, 'shift.' She possibly did not hear me, as she looked adoringly at Oliver, whom she palpably fancied.

Oliver opened his eyes. Catriona stood up and shouted at the errant girl: 'Needy! Get back in your seat! The last thing Oliver needs now is you flirting with him!'

Needy turned towards her slightly, with a look of sweet innocence on her face.

'I'm not flirting,' she said coquettishly, 'Oliver and I are friends. I just want to make sure he's ok.'

Oliver had luxuriant curly black hair. He was looking at her with despair. She stroked the top of his head then, unannounced, he threw up in her lap.

There followed a ghastly fifteen minutes on the edge of a Spanish motorway: Miss Needy changing behind a hedge, supervised by Amanda; Oliver continually apologising; the bus driver swearing and Wyllie, always in charge of puke, ensuring that none adhered to the bus's varied surfaces (I regret to say there was some in the hood of the driver's anorak). Still, I had to try hard to keep my face straight. I liked Oliver very much after that.

Tim

Sometimes young people kill themselves. You know this.

Young people die sometimes when they are still at school. More then than now. One died on the football field, his heart failed, a cheerful, funny boy; one died suddenly at home, something in her brain, a girl of such warmth and energy it was hard to think of her being still; several died of cancer, of course, one a very naughty boy who, in remission, wearing a beanie over his bald head, found places to smoke at school with his girlfriend; a long time ago a boy died at fifteen after his struggle with cystic fibrosis, a clever, clever boy – I see his small, precise handwriting across nearly forty years.

It's always terrible, of course, because you know that their parents will never be whole again and there is nothing you can do. Sometimes I miss not having my own child, but at least I will never go to their funeral.

Early in 2006 I met Tim, who was applying to come to S5 that August. He was coming from Glasgow, but had lived in other places – he had a metropolitan, knowing kind of air. His mother, an elegant, witty woman looked at him with bemusement. I was about fifty, but I knew that had I been sixteen, I would have wanted to be his friend because, though he was a tiny bit up himself ('A *tiny* bit?' says the chorus. 'You're being soft because he's dead'), he was glorious, clever and funny and sharp. He was a skinny boy, all cheekbones and bright eyes, but maybe even then there was a hint of a performance going on, a show for the world. Whatever he was, he was not entirely happy.

Here came Tim to us, almost as brilliant as he thought he was; seemingly exotic in his private life, claiming to be tired on Mondays because he had been in London for the weekend, with his girlfriend who was . . . twenty-eight . . . a model . . . black . . . just publishing her first book. Even though he was just a kid it was almost possible to believe it. Not everyone liked him, and he certainly had a twerpy side to him, but he made a little group of steadfast friends. These were just as clever but less showy boys, who rewarded him with steady loyalty in exchange for his edginess, his risk, his ability to take the piss – he could have done stand-up. He was an English scholar through and through, an artist; though he was indolent and always late and in the wrong place, he wrote beautifully. When the class did Hardy he drew his classmates as characters from *Tess of the d'Urbervilles*; at Christmas he gave us paper baubles for our trees with a photocopy of his face staring wild-eyed on all our festivities. Right at the end of his time with us, one of his art pieces won a prize in a competition and was on display at the National Gallery of Scotland. During the summer holidays after he left, I joined him and his group of friends for a viewing. The rest of us looked at all the pictures, leaving Tim to stand beside his own as if he too were an exhibit. He seemed impossibly arrogant – I think that's what he wanted people to think – but there was something fractured that made you careful with him, and his friends, Jordan and Nick and Eoin, witty intellectuals all, never pressed him too hard lest he shatter.

He went to university, to Manchester, inevitably to do English, and for years I saw him once in a blue moon, almost always at Christmas. Then in March 2013, one of his Edinburgh gang went down to Manchester to celebrate a birthday and spent the evening drinking with Tim; and Tim, who had seemed fine, went home and killed himself, leaving his friend to find out the next day on the train home. Tim had shattered and thus shattered others.

I suppose we just have to let him go, for he wanted to go, and no matter how 'tragic' or 'wasteful' or 'selfish' or 'cruel' it was for him to look at his life then render it void, and no matter how much searching was done in the minds and souls of his family and his pals – and they suffered and suffered – well, what's done is done. We all climbed up Arthur's Seat; there's a place there looking out on the city that's like a wee, private chapel, and there his father, whom none of us had, I think, ever seen before, threw his ashes into the air while mother, stepfather, sister and many others watched, and all his vexatious, funny, clever, annoying, remarkable and unique self blew away in a sudden gust and he spread over Edinburgh, our Tim. If only he had known that he was, in earnest, ours.

I have not been back to that spot on Arthur's Seat, but daily, on my drive to school, I saw the path leading to it and I could not shake Tim away, the bugger, just thinking how fine he might have been as time passed, what he could have become. At Christmas, he still stares from the tree. And our young people are becoming sadder. God help us all.

Pish

I taught in the independent sector and of course a great many of the young people I taught came from 'comfortable' backgrounds. Not all, but most. The vast majority came from happy and secure families – sometimes a little demanding, sometimes a little too involved, but basically they were loved. Not every one, but most. I had a particular affinity with young people who came to private schools from poorer backgrounds, because that was me. School fees yes; holidays no; car no; nice clothes no (emphatically). Aspiration was all, and education was the way to aspire.

I have met legions of great young people – forget brains, I'm talking kindness and compassion and hard work and charm and humour. But there were difficult ones too, and I often found myself hoarding them, the spiky, sad, dissatisfied, depressed kids. I wouldn't really do as a Guidance teacher now, but, since my whole career was an exercise in good timing, in these long decades I served, I was as close to a good Guidance teacher as most who tried. It was an amateur activity in schools then, almost a hobby.

Anyway, this is a story about a bitter, difficult girl, who had, I think, plenty of good reasons for being bitter and difficult, but whom I really liked for her resilience and for her flashes of mordant wit, often aimed at me. Let's call her Pamela. I don't know why but let's do that. Reading this, she will smile and say 'I don't want to be called Pamela, you old git.' Hey, tough. I still see her; so much of her life is still hard – bereavement, injury, illness – but motherhood has softened her. A bit.

So Pamela, Pam, Pammy, you had your very occasional ups and your shedload of downs, but you made it to Sixth Year. Pleasingly, along with a good number of the thirty-three pupils in my Higher class ('bring me your tired, your poor, your huddled masses . . .') of the previous year, you decided to do Advanced Higher. On one particular afternoon I could not, at short notice, take my class, which was the last two periods of the day, and neither could anyone else. I let it be known to the Sixth Year that they should proceed to my room, and read one of the texts they were studying, and that it was not impossible that I might eventually turn up. My friend and colleague Robert Dickson placed a tiny wager with me as to the numbers who would be remaining in the class at the close of the day, and, finding whatever crisis had kept me from them was over, we proceeded together up the turret to the room where they were supposed to be.

Only one of them was there, and that was Pamela. She was pale (she was always pale) and furious. Robert, who was, I think it's fair to say, not a fan, and who didn't know her very well, attempted to engage her in conversation thus: 'So, Mr Wyllie, your class has disappeared, and only Pamela remains. Very good, Pamela.'

She was unmoved, staring at her book; she was about twenty pages into *Jude the Obscure*.

He continued. 'I see you're reading *Jude the Obscure*. I am a big fan of Hardy myself. Are you enjoying it?'

She stopped reading for a moment, turned to him without a hint of a smile, and said, loudly, 'It's pish.' Then went back to her book, while we laughed and laughed. She did not crack a smile.

These days in retirement, when so much new writing exasperates me, I think of Pamela and pish.

Syrians

There is plenty I could say about our Syrians, because taking three refugees into Heriot's was, in truth, probably the best thing I did when I was the Principal. I was only Principal for thirty-nine (long) months, a brief reign, more Lady Jane Grey or Gordon Brown than George III or Mrs Thatcher – though I might be said to share some characteristics with both of them – but if I am to be remembered at all, I would happily be remembered for the Syrians. Saying too much might defeat the purpose of the exercise, to talk about the privations against which they and their families set their faces in order to survive, but something needs to be said.

It was only a little bit my idea; several colleagues and then the two Pupil Councils pushed for something to be done and, as it turned out, not a soul was against it, including the Governors. I doubt if George Heriot knew a lot of Syrians, but we always liked to remember what had motivated him – some urge to help people aspire away from poverty, to set up some late seventeenth-century boys and girls so they could, in time, help their widowed mothers to survive. That was what the school was about, really. And if, by 2016, it had also become an academic, fee-paying institution full of the bright-eyed and cheerful children of the Edinburgh professional classes, there were still plenty of less privileged kids there, the sons and daughters of widows and widowers, plus all of those who didn't pay fees, or paid only a bit. In the great discussion about the charitable status of private schools we never doubted we would pass the test – of course, Heriot's was a charity! Of course! That did not, incidentally, mean that I ever thought that all independent schools were charities or deserved that status, but hey, it would be mean to name names ...

So it came about that after a process involving the City of Edinburgh Council, the Education Department, the Social Work Department and lots of other very helpful people, Lesley and Jo and I sat down to meet our prospective Syrian pupils. We knew we were going to meet several, over a number of days, and we also knew that we had been granted permission by the Governors to take two and to have them at the school, subject to good effort and behaviour, for as long as they could be there. Eventually, at prize-giving, I told the pupils, their parents, the staff and the Governors that we were having three, then explained to the Chairman that, as a teacher of English, I couldn't really be expected to know my numbers. So we took three, and those interviews remain seared in my memory, as so much else dissolves and goes out of focus.

Particularly the first one.

Present were an eleven-year-old boy, smiling genuinely through his confusion; his mother and father; a social worker, whom we went on to meet several times, and who mellowed in her view of independent schools as time passed; a kind and enthusiastic man from the Council, and a Kurdish translator, for this was a Kurdish family. The boy was trying very hard to pretend he spoke English – he liked football, he liked colours (he knew colours), he wanted to be a doctor or a footballer. It was, for all of us, an exercise in cheerful strain. Lesley, the Head of the Junior School, laughed a lot, at nothing in particular. It was not hard to see this was a good lad, open, kind, possibly quite clever. But the answers were all very guarded, and the interview seemed destined to be brief. Just as I was moving to close the discussion, I was conscious that his mother, who had said absolutely nothing, was looking at me hard. I asked the translator to ask her if she wanted to say anything, and she did. The mother began, quietly but determinedly, to tell her son's life story, pausing to let the good-natured old translator catch up.

It was a very, very unhappy story of bombings, destruction, loss of life; moving from the city to the country, which was worse, and then having the 'great luck' to be allowed into a Kurdish refugee camp in, I think, Iraq, where they were at least safe, where the boy spent all day playing football. There was no education of any sort. She concluded by saying that they were very honoured that we were giving up our time to see them, and how much she hoped that her son would be chosen to come to Heriot's. She understood, though, that we were seeing a number of children and could not take them all, and, anyway, all these children were in the same boat, so some would be chosen and some not, and that was fine, and that she wanted God to bless all of them and us too. I thanked her, we stopped and Jo took them out of my office, leaving Lesley and me to cry.

Now I am retired, I use my bus pass. This boy lives on my bus route into town; he stands at the bus stop, like all his peers, in his uniform, listening to his music, nodding his head in time, looking, I imagine, forwards, as he waits to go to school. Maybe someday he will be a doctor, maybe someday he will go back and do good in his troubled land. He has done good here already. Towards the end of his first year with us, in P7, his wise teacher said that one of the other kids had told her she was so pleased that our Syrian boy was in their class, because every day it reminded her how lucky she was.

And the Syrians occasioned kindness. The lovely, clever, slightly older Syrian girl hardly spoke at first, but her charm and her energy won over her classmates. Every year, the new First Year went to Dunoon for an outdoor education bonding session, to which I paid the occasional state visit, always remembering how much the staff already were doing without having to entertain visitors with nice shoes. Anyway, she had gone with great trepidation and had, by all accounts, a great time. On the last night, the occasion of the much anticipated and prepared for 'disco' (the school 'disco' being a feature of the lives of schools unchanged from the actual days when actual people attended discos), one of the other girls asked her guidance teacher if she looked all right.

'Yes,' said the wise lady, 'why?'

'Because Annia didn't have anything to wear for the disco, so I gave her my clothes.'

We also took a much younger boy, a bundle of joy child, I think six when we met him, who was instantly popular, looking round constantly at this new and safe world. Fifteen months after he arrived, I made a ceremonial visit to Junior School Assembly, sang the morning's hymn (which would, no doubt, go something like 'Jesus is a kangaroo, roo, roo'), then watched Lesley do her bit, which was, as always, very good, and actually prepared, unlike some of my own more disparate ramblings at assemblies. It was, she said, the end of the summer, getting colder, and winter was on its way. She had been for a run at the weekend (to clarify, this was on her legs, not a run in the car) and had stood at the top of the hill and looked at the beautiful view and said she would hold that memory in her mind through the winter. Then she asked if anyone would like to share something memorable they had done at the weekend. This being the Junior School, about 98.3 per cent of the kids wanted to do so, and a steady stream of them came up for their fifteen seconds' worth of fame: helped granny make fudge; bought some jeans; went out for a pizza for mum's birthday (mum was forty-three, perhaps a detail best left unshared). Much laughter, much good cheer. Then our by now seven-year-old Syrian came up. 'What did you do at the weekend?' Lesley asked.

'I got a fish and it is golden,' he replied, and I, sitting there in my black gown, was overwhelmed with joy and grief and beauty. This very moment was something to hold next to the heart through the cold winter.

Sausage Rolls in St Andrews

One sunny Saturday I drive two boys to St Andrews to take part in that old university's annual debating competition. I spent lots of Saturdays in various university towns over many years, watching debates while surreptitiously reading the paper, and generally they were good times. These two boys, Ally and Jonny, are twelve, and they are debaters and thus dependable conversationalists. It is the first time they have been to a competition, and they prattle away merrily for all the long rolling distance from the A9 to St Andrews.

As soon as we get there it becomes clear I have made a mistake. I thought this competition was for S1 and S2, but in fact it is for S1, S2 and S3. My skinny boys seem tiny and, in the first round they are smashed about by some big girls from Aberdeen, some big girls from Glasgow and some rough boys from Lanarkshire (well, rough is relative in debating terms . . .). They come fourth out of four teams. The presiding judge is not very nice to them. When I talk to them afterwards, in my vague coaching style, they are upset and I apologise for the age mix-up. They are not pleased with me, and I wonder whether it might be best just to give up and take them home; they are scared of being further squashed in the next room, slightly tearful even.

Then, a miracle. A lovely, clever, smiling St Andrews student takes them in hand; she had watched the first debate, she says, and thought they were really good, given their age. Between us, we coax them to do another round. I am fairly sure they will do better, because this will be a room of teams who came last in the first round. I hold my breath, put the paper away and concentrate on willing them to be confident. To be honest, I would settle for them not actually crying. The lovely student settles herself beside me and beams positivity at them, and, glory be, they do much better. The judges are really effusive this time, comment on their youth and place them second. All the bitterness of the first round is gone, Jonny and Ally are very, very happy and I am greatly relieved.

There is a break for lunch. Eschewing the university's horrible sandwiches, I take them to Greggs, which has a seated area. It is very busy, so I tell them to claim a table, then, mindful of the school's Healthy Eating Policy, buy three sausage rolls, three French fancies and three cans of Fanta.

When I find them, they are talking to an old woman who is on her own. They are telling her about their day. I sit down, they introduce me, and then they talk some more. When they run out of things to say, I ask her how her own day is going. She tells us that it is the first time she has been into the town since her husband died, a few months before. Her family have been very good to her, she says, but they are far away, and she knows she needs to get out or she will be lonely. For the second time that day, my two boys look like they might cry. They ask about her grandchildren and she is visibly pleased; they ask about St Andrews, about her garden, about her life. She tells them about her husband, warmly and kindly. Eventually though, I have to say that it's time for us to cross the road back into the university union. We rise and say our goodbyes.

'Excuse me,' she says to me, as the boys make for the door, 'what school are you from?'

'George Heriot's in Edinburgh.'

'Well,' she says, 'that must be a great school.'

On Monday, at Assembly, I tell this story, and my voice breaks at the end. Once again, I am caught out by the never-ending kindness of the young. These boys must be twenty-seven now, but there may be a very old lady who lives near St Andrews who thinks of them from time to time.

Reflection

Drama/Crisis

When I was eight, my class teacher was Beryl Buteux. We quickly learnt how to pronounce her name. It was not 'buttocks', it was 'b-you-toe', though hours of fun were had by calling her Mrs Buttocks behind her back. She was, of every teacher I ever came into contact with, the one who most resembled Jean Brodie. Beryl was an elegant and attractive woman, of large gestures and colourful dress who, exotically, was English. She was not exactly a 'crank', but we spent an inordinate amount of time – which, back then, we loved – doing expressive arts work, mainly by undertaking the group construction of what I thought were 'college pictures'. Collaaajjj pictures, she eventually explained.

Miss Buteux was very keen on drama, and we did plenty in class. When I was in P7 she asked me to audition for the part of the little winsome dweeb, the eponymous Oliver of the musical version of *Oliver Twist*. She guessed, I think, that my sweet little voice and blond hair would make a success of 'Where Is Love?' – possibly less with my peers and more with their grannies. Alas, I didn't even get the chance to try out, because my mother forbade it on the grounds that we lived too far away and it would be a hassle. So that was that for drama at school, except for a melodrama in sixth year when, as I recall, I played the part of a whore. This was a less obvious bit of character casting.

Entrants to the teaching profession now are often advised to 'say no for the first year'. The idea is that you spend your time honing the perfect lesson, continuing at every opportunity with your professional development and reflecting on your practice, so that you become a 'reflective practitioner'.

Now in 1980, none of this was current thinking. I do remember really, really planning a lesson once, during my teaching practice, that

I was to teach in front of Squadron Leader (retd) J. W. Richardson, the much-feared teacher of English and Housemaster at DSMC.

The context of this lesson was not encouraging. The previous week I had observed Jock teaching a poem by Norman MacCaig, that over-taught Scottish silver poet, one of the ones about being on a hill ... sigh. Jock was very keen on MacCaig and very keen on hills. I think it's fair to say that his approach to literary criticism was a mite didactic: 'Now, look at this image – "the Joseph-coated frogs" – Ancona, tell me why that's a great image.'

Simon Ancona, a demure and thoughtful lad, thought a bit. 'I don't think it's a great image, sir. It depends on you knowing about Joseph and his dreamcoat.'

Jock shook his head and looked at me.

'Mr Cameron?' Honestly, that's what he called me – I'm not sure if it was unintentional, or meant to demonstrate that I was only a short distance along the way from them to him.

'Well,' I said, 'I think I agree with Simon.'

'Right,' responded Jock, 'you teach them the lesson next week.' In my memory he threw the book at me, but that may not be true.

My planned lesson was to be on another dreary poem by MacCaig, and so fearful of Jock was I that I got a friend who knew MacCaig to phone him so I could check something. I even took in a visual aid – a tiny photo of the Empire State Building (yes, it was *that* poem). At the end Jock said I should stay behind so he could 'debrief' me. I had no idea what that would involve – but with great relief, I realised that it meant he wanted to talk to me about the lesson, which had suggested to him that I might turn out to be a good teacher. This was praise indeed. From that point on, I didn't really plan lessons.

And as for 'professional development', I was never very into that, and nobody who knows me could conceivably say I was ever reflec-tive about anything really. So, 'saying no for the first year', even if it had been thought of at the time, would not have been my practice. I said yes, yes and yes. I supervised discos, I went to cheer on sports teams and I ended up helping with drama. Though I have never loved theatre like I love cinema or cake, helping with drama was one of the best things I did in my career. I now say this to young teachers: saying yes tends to make you more popular, and saying yes a lot can make you invaluable. Consider the holy grail of the permanent contract the next time you say no to helping with the Duke of Edinburgh's Award so you can stay at home and work on your lifelong learning all weekend. Or all your life.

Helping with drama in my early years meant working with Johnny Rintoul. Johnny was a very kind and hospitable man, and he and his wife Alyson, also a drama teacher, were . . . dramatic. The drama boys (supplemented with actual girls from the Mary Erskine School) were well looked after by Johnny, and he by them; for he did on occasion lose his temper, and with an imperious and commanding tone, designed to reach the back stalls, would say 'Take my name off the programme, Mr Wyllie' and storm off to the staffroom. This would be on a wet night in November in the assembly hall, and there would be, at this stage, no programme anyway. So the boys and girls and I carried on for five minutes, then I would take myself off to the staffroom to assist in Johnny's recomposure. After a wee bit he would return, and everyone would be good as gold until it happened again a fortnight later.

I did various things, mostly badly, but I was willing. Once I was prompting during a production of Arthur Miller's little known one act play *Incident at Vichy* – there are, I should say, reasons why it is little known. Prompting is very boring. So I had slightly lost concentration when silence fell among the actors, and I found a lovely talented girl called Alice Steuart staring at me from the stage. I smiled back, then suddenly, with a wave of clammy consciousness, remembered I was prompting. The script said: 'she takes a mirror from her bag', so I said 'mirror'.

'Mirror? Mirror!' she muttered, then Johnny shouted 'In your bag'. No bag, though, for it was lying on the table beside me. I was also in charge of props. She came off and re-entered with the bag, to some amusement from the crowd, the tragic tone of the piece somewhat impaired. Johnny forgave me . . . quite quickly, really.

Johnny also taught the drama lessons, and given he was the expert, we mere mortal English teachers went to watch him teach. It's a different world, the real teaching of drama by drama teachers; it's no more for an English teacher to do than if they were to teach Art or PE or Chemistry, God help us.

So one day I went to see Johnny teaching in the big hall, an S2 class which included two identical twins. I remember almost nothing about these boys, except they were really identical, said very little and were Latin American ballroom dancing champions. Yes, that does stick in my mind.

Johnny, pleased, I think, to have the company of his young acolyte, began: 'OK, I want you to imagine you are a Spanish conquistador!'

He then checked to ensure that they all had a rough notion of what that was.

'So you have landed your ship on an unknown tropical beach, and you disembark. You are very grand, clad in velvet and armour, looking at the world through your helmet, because you have no idea what might be waiting for you – animals, other humans – then slowly, from the jungle, onto the beach, there emerges a single native, a young man, wearing only a loincloth...'

He paused to allow this faintly homoerotic image to settle in his pupils' minds, then turned to one of the twins.

'So, Bill – or are you Ben? If you were that conquistador' (all four syllables exquisitely enunciated) 'how would you feel?'

Bill/Ben shifted uncomfortably, now more or less literally in the limelight.

'Hot?' he muttered.

Eventually, encouraged by Johnny, I struck out on my own into the world of Middle School drama, and for four happy years in a row I directed a musical, with a cast of thousands from S1 and S2 at DSMC and the Mary Erskine School. I worked with Dave Wright, a witty and affable Glaswegian who taught brass at the school, and his wife Irene, a choreographer. Irene was a lovely woman but not to be crossed, so discipline in our vast casts was maintained, with Irene just very occasionally losing her temper quite spectacularly, while Dave and I tried not to giggle.

Anyone who wanted could be in these shows, but we auditioned everybody who came along, just to see if they could do a big part. I remember Danny. Danny was a cheerful lunk of a boy who turned up for his audition five minutes late, in a day when we had been auditioning for hours and hours. They had to read for me, sing for Dave and dance for Irene. In five minutes for each audition. Twelve an hour, about sixteen or seventeen hours over three days. It was hellish, but we never stopped laughing, and, of course, we found lots of talent. And Danny.

In he came, leaving the door open.

'Shut the door please,' said Irene, which he did.

'Now, Danny, which part do you want to read for?' The bodyguard, I thought; the policeman – he's a nice lad, we can give him a line. Make his granny proud.

'Shakespeare,' he said, this being the main role, more or less on the stage throughout.

'OK, have you learnt the lines?' There were seventy-two words which they were supposed to have learnt if they wanted to try for this big part.

'No, can I use the book?' Yes, he could, but he didn't have his copy. I gave him mine. He found the place and read. Badly.

Dave wrote 'Can't act at all' on Danny's piece of paper, then quickly moved him on to singing. He sang the snippet of the catchy wee tune Dave and I had written. We were a bit like Elton and Bernie. A small bit.

'Can't sing at all,' Dave wrote.

Then Irene got up, bless her, and did a wee dance while Dave played the piano. This was a wee dance they had all done the previous week, for an hour or so, and it lasted thirty seconds. Danny could not copy her, and basically just stood.

'Can't dance.'

'That's great, Danny,' I said. 'Can I just check – if you don't get a part, are you happy to be in the chorus?'

'Yes,' he said, beaming happily. Then he left, leaving the door open behind him.

Dave wrote, 'Can't even shut the fucking door.'

We put Danny in the back row of the chorus, but in every performance he somehow or other got to the front.

We did four shows. *Helen Come Home*, all boys, in Portobello Town
Hall, featured a weird cross-dressing beauty competition; altogether
strange. The video looks like a Satanic ritual is taking place. Then *Tin
Pan Ali*, better because we brought in the girls. These two musicals
were by Jeremy James Taylor, and they worked pretty well, but Dave
and I thought we could do better, and so we wrote *Where There's a
Will*. This was a very, very silly thing, set in the present day, with Will
Shakespeare played by a girl, having a romance with Anne Hathaway,
who is in the chorus line of Shakespeare's latest show, in a theatre
owned by a Mafia boss, and which features a song called 'It's a Very
Hard Job Being a Queen', performed by a boy dressed as Queen
Elizabeth the First. I am just going to say, despite its astonishing
lightweight forgettability, the first night of that play was one of the
happiest times of my life. The evening was capped by a conversation
with the father of one of the cast, a girl playing a 'tart with a heart',
who advised the innocent Anne about men, and who ended the performance dressed as a nun. This gentleman approached me, identified
me and hugged me, saying 'Mr Wyllie, you are a fucking genius.' And,
for about five minutes, that's how I felt. 'Where there's a will, where
there's a will, where there's a will, there's a waaaaaaaay.' I wonder how
many of that cast, now in their forties, can still hear that song echoing
from a distant time, in the theatres of their memory.

The lead in that show was an astonishingly talented girl called
Jenny Hutchinson. She grew into an amazing all-rounder – academic,
sporty, singing and dancing and the most positive, helpful individual
to boot, though she never actually needed booting. At this point she
was thirteen. On the first night she stood beside me waiting to go on,
and I succeeded in leaning on a door which then shut her hand in the
jamb. I will never forget the noise she made – like a cat in distress. I
thought I had at least broken a finger or two, and was ready to leap
on stage and pretend to be a thirteen-year-old girl. But she just went
on, tears of pain in her eyes, and got on with it. This year I saw her at
a school show at Heriot's watching her daughter perform, and I was

able to tell her talented lassie this story, which she already knew, of course. Seeing them, mother and daughter, made me feel . . . profound, in some way, for about three minutes or so.

The phrase 'those were different times' has been ill-used as a justification by all sorts of perverts, but the world of school drama really was different then. In 1991, this time with Roger Askew who was Director of Music at DSMC, I wrote another show called *Custer's Last Band*, which was politically incorrect on so many levels I should really be ashamed. To wit, it was about General Custer, but the premise was that the Battle of Little Big Horn was in fact a singing competition between the US Cavalry, led by Custer, and the Indians, a tribe called the Yellow Bellies, who had a medicine man called Boot the Chemist (I thought that was really funny. Nobody else did). The Cavalry's song in the competition is a mock country epic, which includes the lines 'My mama was a drunkard, and my daddy was a lady of the night', and 'Mama had fourteen children, and all but me were blind'. Custer has a fiancée, with a demented father, but also has a girlfriend called Scarlett O'Hairy, who is a burlesque singer in a bar. This part was played by Madeleine Worrall, who has gone on to a great career as an actor, but I cannot imagine she lists this early role on her CV. The part of the Indian chief was played gloriously by a very camp child called Craig. His first appearance involved him bursting out of a tepee (there were a number of jokes involving this word) because he has been awakened by the loud ululations of several of his tribesmen (one of them is now very, very senior in the University of Oxford). Craig, resplendent in a marvellous full length headdress, emerged and said 'What is all this noise?' like a prepubescent Frankie Howerd (wot ees alll this noooyysse???). The audience laughed for two minutes solid, then laughed at the way they had laughed, then laughed at Craig, who was standing stock still on stage, amazed at his capacity to make people happy. At the interval I met his mother on the stairs of the George Square Theatre.

'A star is born,' I exulted.

'That's one way of putting it,' she observed, thoughtfully.

When school drama is bad, it's a drag and a half. Teachers need to remember that the audience is there to see their child or their grandchild or their nephew or niece, and if they really, truly enjoy their evening, that is a blessing. So it either has to be really good, or short. The best thing I ever saw on a school stage was my friend Iain Scott's production of *My Fair Lady*, which was simply perfect, with sets so astonishing that the audience clapped every time the curtains opened. Fabulous. Heads and parents should never forget that 'doing' the school show is the most difficult thing a teacher can do. Honestly, beside it, a weekly rugby practice and a match on a Saturday is a walk in the park; my rugby practices (see above) actually were walks in the park, in fact.

In the penultimate stage of my career, when I was the Head Teacher of the Senior School at Heriot's, I assisted Chalmers Neil with several of his musical productions. Chalmers was a kind, gossipy, able man and Head of Maths, and he loved musical theatre. Several of his productions were very good, with casts who became attuned eventually to Chalmers' distinctive – and mathematical – approach to choreography. I did the book, i.e. the acting, which is sometimes rather neglected in school musicals, and I enjoyed it, always feeling very appreciated by the stressed but optimistic Mr Neil.

In 2002 Chalmers decided that the show should be *Crazy for You* and set about auditioning, excusing me from the process with the argument that I had more important things to be doing; I suspect it was more to do with control. But one lunchtime he caught me in the playground to say that he just couldn't find anybody to play the lead male role, Bobby Child, and that because this was such a big part, which involved real skills in singing, dancing and acting, the whole thing would have to be called off, etc., etc. He was in despair, because there was only one audition left, for a senior pupil called Emun Mohammadi. Now, I knew and really liked Emun, whom I was teaching that year, and he was reading Tennessee Williams in my class really well, but I had no idea if he could sing or dance. Poor Chalmers, despairing, went off to meet him.

Well, reader, he could sing and he could dance and he got the part, and got Chalmers smiling again (thank God!). And really, the whole thing, after months of painful flat rehearsal with missing kids and lines not learnt, and young people failing to remember their Chalmers code numbers for song 17, came together pretty well. On the first night, the curtain opened on Emun, leaning on a lamp post reading a paper and smoking a pretend cigarette. He read, he smoked and nothing happened. He smoked, he read and nothing happened. The lead girl, played by the irrepressible Nicola Irvine, was supposed to appear but didn't. Another few moments passed, then through the sound system came Nicola's unmistakable voice saying 'I just . . . can't . . . get it oooonnn', and it became clear there was a mishap. So Emun nodded at the conductor, the band began to play the first tune and Emun danced until Nicola appeared, as if he had been doing that sort of thing professionally forever. His first night of his first show.

Emun became an actor, changed his name to Emun Elliott, did a lot of stage and TV with lots of famous people, and one October not long ago we watched him on Broadway in a play by Tennessee Williams. All my life's a circle, as the New Seekers so memorably sang in 1972.

Sketches of Carbisdale

I am basically not that keen on the outdoors – if God had wanted us to have fresh air, why did He give us windows? When people say how much they love the countryside I am always reminded of the opening of *The Big Chill*, Jeff Goldblum doing up his fly, looking around and saying, 'I love the outdoors. It's one big toilet.' I am really a city boy: I like shops and cinemas and restaurants; I am reassured by the presence of large crowds of people; I like central heating and double glazing and hotels with good showers.

Once a year, for eight days, every boy in the third year at Daniel Stewart's and Melville College and every girl in the third year of the Mary Erskine School for Girls went to Carbisdale Castle in Sutherland. In the early years, before my time, they went by special trains, arriving at the tiny station in Ardgay, then humping their stuff up the considerable distance to the castle. By the Eighties the journey was made easier, and a fleet of buses took us direct from Edinburgh.

Yes, I say 'us'. It was clear to me that anyone who was anyone on the staff went to Carbisdale. I did not like being shut out of the camaraderie and stories when they returned and, in any case, there was a role for me. This was not leading groups of children up Munros, no. It was not demonstrating the construction of a bivouac made from a canoe, no. It was, in fact, to provide the commentary on a bus tour – vaguely centred around the history and geography of the area – which cleverly helped the time to pass for a busful of children on the day's journey from Carbisdale Castle to Strathpeffer Youth Hostel, the other outdoor centre that was used. The Youth Hostel at Strathpeffer was, for years and years, presided over by Cliff Porteous from the Chemistry department, who always in some ways seemed to me to be the younger brother my father did not have. Cliff loved these trips; I have a photo of him sitting in the sun between busloads of kids looking blissfully happy. Indeed, he observed, these projects would be perfect if no children were involved.

The bus tour was, compared to the tremendously butch things that most of my colleagues were doing, a positively effeminate activity, but I enjoyed it every year for years. One central reason for this was that the leading organiser of the wee tour was Dr Iain Scott of the History department at the girls' school, and he is my best friend now and has been for . . . getting on for forty years, since I met him at a briefing about Carbisdale. Anything that involved the company of this kind, warm and funny man, who wears his considerable learning so lightly, was bound to be a pleasure. When I moved from DSMC to Heriot's I missed many things, particularly at first, but Carbisdale lingered long in my blood, and eventually Heriot's too went there, until in the bad winter of 2010, the Castle, owned and operated as a Youth Hostel, was so badly damaged that it was closed down. It is, I believe, being converted into a luxury private residence, but not for me: too many ghosts, not to mention the considerable distance to the nearest Waitrose.

Carbisdale became almost a ritual event for the staff who went: the same uncomfortable sleeping quarters, enlivened by the horrors of colleagues snoring; always being slightly damp; the weird smells of the castle, particularly the grim showers. What I remember most is spending time with the staff of the Mary Erskine School – Paddy Forbes making bread and butter pudding for fifty because I was a bit down one day and she asked me what I would like; Sally Duncanson talking about how handsome the boys were, even the ugly ones; Doreen Waugh, cheerfully explaining the origin of Gaelic names; and May Burns, who was the Deputy Head and seemed to the children to be a hundred years old, despite her evident stamina. Ah, Miss Burns briefing the children before their night under canvas, always I think slightly nervous that the boys would riot: 'Do not ever set a fire inside a tent. That would be very foolish and dangerous. Each tent and its associated equipment costs the school £189. Plus you would be burned to a crisp, and that would be a tragedy.' I always loved it that the cost came before the loss of life. She was a fine woman.

There are many stories about Carbisdale. I could tell you about the staff crossing the rail bridge to get to the pub and, on one occasion, almost not getting across in time; I could tell you about the glue-sniffing (that wasn't the staff); I could tell you about sex and orienteering (neither, I hasten to add, was that); and I could tell you about the exploding toilet, but here are some tales at least.

Hill Fort

I have said before that I don't know much about History, but on these projects I was reassured by the fact that Doc Scott knew everything, and of course that meant he had to be right there in case of queries. On the very first day of my very first Carbisdale, the afternoon activity – not on the bus – was to tour Strathpeffer, commencing with a visit to the 'famous' Iron Age hill fort. It was a blithesome day; I had the grand company of my new friend, and I set about getting to know the girls, while he, a teacher at the girls' school, talked to the boys. We climbed the relevant hill, which was extensive, and two or three of the girls and I were well in front. We arrived at what appeared to be the summit, and I, expecting the hill fort to resemble a more modest Edinburgh Castle (I was looking forward to browsing in the gift shop) looked to Iain Scott for help. He was ambling up the mountain in the company of Geoff, a red-haired boy who was constantly cheerful and talked non-stop.

'Where is the hill fort, Dr Scott?' I bellowed.

'You are standing on it.'

This was my first year there. That year someone gave me a lift home after the bus had deposited us back at the school. I remember getting out of their car outside my flat and thinking how loud the world was.

Distillery

Part of the bus tour involved a visit to a distillery. We went to various different ones, but my favourite was Glenmorangie in Tain. I still love Glenmorangie, and when I drink it I am inevitably taken back to these days in May long ago. The manager, an ancient man called Mr McGregor, whose grandfather had sat on the board of the company until he was ninety-two, enjoyed the company of our young people, which must have broken up the long distillery days where nothing happened; only the coopers appeared actually to do any work. He would take us round and patiently explain, in his beautiful Highland voice, the process by which this astonishing luxury product was made, having begun by telling them that the whisky was called 'Glenmorangie, as in "orange"'. At the end, he would give the same little speech each time: 'Boys and girrells, you have been vera, vera well-behaved. If you proceed back to the bus, I will take your teeaacherrs upstairs and give them some pencils for you.'

Thus the children, further admonished to behave well by the teeaacherrs, went back to the bus and to the care of the driver, and we proceeded upstairs, at about three in the afternoon, where Mr McGregor would pour us each a large whisky, adding, from the Glenmorangie-branded jug, a teaspoonful of water. There was, of course, no time to appreciate this properly, given that the noise from the bus would grow till it was unavoidable, but it would have been rude to refuse. We would knock it back, accept the pencils – and a miniature or two for the driver – and run back to the bus. The kids, of course, worked out what the pencil ritual was about, particularly when, on one occasion, two of the lady staff entertained them with a singalong of great hits of the Fifties, with which the young people could not, of course, sing along. Generally, I dropped off to sleep for the remaining forty-five minutes to Strathpeffer, deaf to the rammy.

Part of the procedure at Glenmorangie was that the kids got a taste of the whisky. Mr McGregor, after ritually asking my permission each time, would uncork a barrel and lower into it a copper vacuum pump, a thing of beauty, which he jiggled and thus filled with whisky – this, of course, was much stronger than the stuff we eventually drink from the bottle.

Now, I cannot imagine that any teacher at the present day would allow their precious charges even a sip, but we did then. On the very first of these occasions he handed the pump to a boy called Rory and said 'Now try that.' Rory was the essence of goodness, a wee blond boy who almost certainly has never, ever done anything wrong even now he's forty-eight. Rory was young for the year and very obedient. He lifted the copper tube to his lips and began to gulp it down, clearly, we realised in retrospect, believing that each child would be drinking what must have amounted to half a pint or so of proof whisky. He had, I suppose, had a couple of mouthfuls before I screamed at him to stop. Mr McGregor was momentarily irritated, believing Rory was being wide, but I was able to assure him that Rory was so narrow he barely existed. However, by the time we got back on the bus, Rory was cheerfully pissed, and, under the pretext of him 'feeling a bit sick', and having sworn the other children to secrecy on the basis that Mr Porteous would be angry with him – Cliff believing that more or less all children were immensely wide – we got him off to bed for a couple of hours. It was a tale for him to tell when he wanted to.

Anthony's Clothes

When I went to DSMC as a student teacher, my colleagues in the English department were all very good to me, but Elizabeth Dorward, one of the few women on the staff of the school and the only one in the department, took me right under her wing. She was a confident, happy, clever woman, a Highland lady, thin and constantly laughing. She adored the boys, particularly those in her House, for she was a Housemaster. This was an unusual thing in 1980, to have a woman in pastoral and disciplinary charge of eighty boys in a boys' school, and it was testament to the fact that Robin Morgan, the Principal – and many of the other men on the staff – loved her. I came late to that game – after only a few years of my being there she was diagnosed with cancer, and after an actual struggle, an honest fight, she died in 1987 and I lost a real friend.

But all of this was to come; in my first year going to Carbisdale my pastoral duties were with her House, which meant it was a joy. I remember her taking me for afternoon tea in a huge old-fashioned hotel in Strathpeffer; I have a vivid memory of huge scones and thick cream, though I don't recall exactly which part of my professional duties this represented.

The boys in Tay House, which was Elizabeth's domain, were a little different: gentlemanly, charming, debonair. Not camp, of course, for that would have been going too far, but not brutal, softer, gentler. They were, at Carbisdale, at fourteen years of age, maybe a tiny bit more calm than the others, being with this kind and confident substitute mother who, as her deputy on this occasion, had cheerful, silly me, who was, shall we say, not a role model in the butch stakes.

Elizabeth was very keen on cleanliness and tidiness; she was also competitive. Dormitories were inspected nightly, and she expected that her boys would keep their two rooms spick and span, which broadly they did rather than risk her disappointment, a more potent disciplinary weapon than any amount of shouting. At the end of the eight days – long, happy days – Elizabeth was determined that her boys should take home tidy bags, and thus please their mothers, so offered a prize for the neatest packing. Just before we left, we wandered about the two rooms examining the boys' luggage, and decided that Anthony had won.

This was a surprise. Anthony was a rotund boy, the youngest of a family inclined to rotundness. He had found many of the activities

110

difficult, and, though generally of very cheery disposition, had moaned frequently, while also developing the habit of asking lots of questions, none of them to do with anything educational, mainly concerned with mealtimes and when, precisely, the bus for home would depart. One did not expect him to be able to pack so neatly, but his case was far and away the winner. Elizabeth, with an encouraging and cheerful smile, made a little speech to the effect that all of us were good at something. Some of us could abseil down the side of a cliff face (not her or me, she added) and some could pack well. She then gave Anthony his prize, which was probably a Mars bar, that staple of outdoor education which, I suspect, would have lasted about thirty seconds in Anthony's practiced hands. We left the dormitory, perhaps aware of a vague and unusual air of discontent among the boys.

We were pursued, at a discreet distance, by the Tay House captain, a really sharp and kind boy who had a shining future ahead of him.

'Mrs Dorward,' he began, 'em ... we don't think it's fair that Anthony won the prize for packing.'

'Well, it was a bit of a surprise, I admit, but his was clearly the best?' I nodded in agreement.

'Yes but, you see ...' he continued, 'he never unpacked. I don't think he's ever opened his case.'

The horror quickly sank in and Mrs D nearly passed out. Eight days of outdoor education. Up hill, down dale, in canoes, on buses, camping, Anthony had not changed clothes; the outdoor waterproofs had no doubt just gone on top. Elizabeth paled.

'Do you know if he showered?'

'I don't think so, Miss ...'

Harris Is Transformed

Harris came to Carbisdale in my House group. He was a difficult young man, and I had to defend him against a lot of criticism from his teachers: he was rude, bad-tempered, lazy. His parents lived abroad and he boarded in the small boarding-house adjacent to the school. I think he felt that nobody loved him and, truth to tell, he did not conform to any picture of a loveable child; he was suspicious of any attempt to cheer him up, and even the kindest boys were rebuffed. I did not look forward to taking him to Carbisdale, and sure enough he was bitching about it for weeks before. He rarely smiled; he may well have been bullied; he trusted no one.

Each house was paired with a clan from the girls' school, travelled with them and did every activity with them, often including ones that were not part of the outdoor education programme. Initially, of course, coming as they did from single-sex schools, the boys tried to be hard and the girls shrieked a lot, but that mainly passed quickly, and everyone settled into a very tolerable symbiosis. And, of course, the girls and their teachers had few preconceptions about the boys, and vice versa. As a result, what happened was that two or three of the girls saw Harris initially, I think, as a sort of project – we have to remember that fourteen-year-old girls, in general, seem about three years older than fourteen-year-old boys. For these girls Harris had no backstory, no reputation, and because the bus journey there took hours and hours, by the time we arrived wearily at the Castle he had friends, and for those seven days of activities, and for the long journey home, he was very, very happy. 'I like that Harris,' said glorious Linda, who was the clan mistress I worked with, on the bus home, 'and so do the girls'. True enough, when he smiled and laughed you could almost see what he would become – a friend, a boyfriend, a husband, a father. I worried much less about Harris from that point on. Some boys, possibly all boys, but definitely some boys, should never go to single-sex schools.

Assemblies

1969

The First Year sat upstairs in the balcony of the Senior Hall for Assembly, at first excited about the new journey into secondary education – though still wearing shorts – and then awed into silence at the procession every morning of the school prefects (it was a quirk of Heriot's tradition that even the staff stood up when the prefects entered the Hall; this nonsense didn't stop until 1993). Eventually, of course, we students were neither excited nor awed, just bored. Hymn, prayer, reading from the Bible; then, on good days, the Headmaster, the fearsome intellectual Dr Dewar, would address us. I sat with my friend David, an eminently middle-class, actually rather posh boy, my friendship with whom was much encouraged by my mother, for David was polite and very clever. I liked him for many reasons, one of which was that he had an astonishingly immature sense of humour, and I could make him laugh. There was, at that time, a radio broadcaster called Freddie Grisewood (he presented *Any Questions?* for decades) and it was my habit to say his name in a peculiar voice in order to make David laugh, which it always did. The word 'teapot' had the same effect. I should tell you that he has had a very distinguished career but still laughs at very silly things.

Anyway, I don't know if Freddie or teapots were in the mix of our whispered conversation on this particular day, but at Assembly's dreary close, a PREFECT appeared and said 'Dr Dewar wants to see you now. You were talking in Assembly.' AAAAAARRRGGGGHH! He then led us in total ignominy from the Hall to the staffroom. This was a brief enough journey, during which David – rugged though he no doubt is – sobbed. For me, the issue wasn't about Dr Dewar, scared though I was, but about my mother, who would, I knew, hear of this from my big brother, who was himself one of the sainted prefects.

Dr Dewar was uniformly known as 'Dome' because of his shiny bald head, which he kept concealed under a mortar board. We stood for a moment surveying the staffroom, with its important seventeenth-century Scottish fireplaces, up the chimneys of which we would gratefully have climbed, until Dome arrived. He swept in, and the staff paused, last-minute coffee in hand, to watch us be dispatched. He took off his mortar board and laid it carefully on the table. David looked like he might die, but I knew my real punishment would come later.

'You were talking in Assembly.' This was not a question.

'If you are caught talking in Assembly again, I will thrash you.' There was a heavy emphasis on the 'thrash' word. There was not a particle of warmth in it, but hey ho, that was that. We would not talk at Assembly again (well, in theory) and he had let us go, out into the crisp sunlight of the Quadrangle. We hurried to class.

All day I thought about my mother.

I was the first home, as was usually the case. I knew what I had to do. For years I had told lies when in trouble because I was scared of my mother, but eventually – it was a painful process, alleviated by my father's counsel – I understood that the lying was the thing she hated most, more than the overflowing washing machine, or the missing selection box, or the hanky covered in dog shit (don't ask). It was a lovely day and, weirdly, our house had a little putting green, which was my father's pride and joy, so I was pretending to be putting when the car carrying both my parents entered the garage. They emerged.

I didn't wait.

'I got into trouble today at school and was taken to Dr Dewar with David because we were talking in Assembly. I won't do it again [until Thursday] and I'm really sorry.'

'Did he punish you?' asked my dad, clearly aware that this would indicate the gravity of the crime.

'No, not really, but he said he would if it happened again.'

'You just never shut up, you have to learn to keep quiet,' said my mother, but kindly enough. They didn't say this, but I think they were pleased that I had just come out with it.

Things were pleasingly normal. The sun continued to shine. My dad came out for a putt. Then Jimmy came home. He just couldn't wait.

'He got into trouble for talking at Assembly,' was his opening greeting to his family, at the end of the long day for us all.

'We know. He told us. Don't clype on your brother,' said my mother, and whacked him.

Ah, bliss.

1970

Dr Dewar again, but really, really angry. Some boy had been rude to Alec, the Head Janitor. The boy himself had clearly been slowly eviscerated, his internal organs spread before him on a fire no doubt set by Alec himself. I was not sympathetic. I could not imagine how such a thing could have happened – Alec was a quiet, dignified man, not a cheery soul like Sandy, his assistant. He lived in the Head Janitor's house, a source of some wonder to the boys, for its door was set into the Flodden Wall (1514) which formed part of the boundary of the school. This was, of course, in the days before planning regulations.

What we did not know about Alec, which Dr Wm. McL. Dewar was now telling us, was that he had been a Japanese prisoner-of-war, and had suffered terribly. Dome spelt this out, that this skinny pale old man had been through horrors for his country, and now some twerpy spoilt boy had been rude to him. He was furious and, of course, he was right. Alec, close to retirement, was clearly not a well man, and whatever had been said had clearly been enough to cause him to complain. The rest of what the consequences would be was written in an old book called 'Respect the Janitor', composed a very long time ago, and something of a gospel in any school.

However, the horror of this was only intensified by the pigeon which was flying about in the Hall, something which only happened this once in all the time I was there. I think, probably, Dr Dewar was the only person unaware of it, consumed as he was with fury. He was bright red and, as the pigeon made a sally well above his head, he took his mortar board off. No one moved; no one said a word. The stuff of legend was in front of us, but I'm glad, really, that the pigeon did not crap on Dome, not that it would have stopped him. The pigeon may have been just bird-witted enough to realise that something serious was happening, something about integrity, something about kindness, something about loyalty; in any case, there were plenty of guns in the Cadets' armoury.

2011

There are lots of problems with school assemblies, but the main one, of course, is religion. I have never really been religious, which is hard when you have had my career. Being made to plot the journeys of

St Paul on squared paper in the chapel as a pupil didn't help. Then all these mornings, boy and man, for years and years singing hymns and being told to pray. Really.

Now I have reached a stage in my life where I see religion as being like golf. I was once at a dinner where I was sitting next to a large, rather deaf, old man, a stranger, who, as the starter was served, turned to me and said, 'DO YOU GOLF?' Startled, I giggled nervously and said 'no', and that completed my entire conversation with him. A year later, at the same function, I sat next to a woman whom I did know. I asked her why she and her husband had decided to come to Edinburgh. 'Because God sent us,' she replied. I really didn't know what to say, and let her, too, turn to her other companion. Pleasingly, I had a doctor on the other side with whom I could talk about illness, which I always enjoy.

Religion and golf. Two things in which significant minorities of the population are interested and, if you are interested in them, you tend to be very interested. Willy, in the paper shop at the top of my road, judges each day a success or failure on the basis of his likely access to the golf course. Similarly, there are people for whom God never seems terribly far away. This is, of course, the right of golfers and of the pious, but it has to be said that young people are never invited at 8.30 am to practise their putting, presumably because most of them don't golf. However, in some schools they are expected to sing hymns (few do, unless threatened, their dreary drone a daily horror for music teachers); pray (shutting your eyes is nice); listen to the Bible (much good sense there and, to be fair, schools mainly shy away from the flaying, the misogyny, the homophobia and the other really silly bits).

But stop and think and it's just peculiar. In an average school, the very vast majority don't go to church; it isn't that they are atheists or agnostics or have lost their faith, they're just not bothered. Schools shouldn't therefore pander to the parents or the staff or the governors who are still doing a round every day on God's golf course.

I've nothing against the idea that, on some mornings, our young people should be given important things to think about. I even think it's good if, on occasion, a person from some religious group explains what they think and why; but we're surely well past assuming that some padre has the (God-given) right to monopolise the minds of our kids. In any case, it just turns them off.

As a small boy I went to Sunday School in our village. My mother went to church about three times a year, to keep her toe in Heaven's door, and so we were to go to Sunday School. My brother became a Sunday School teacher, I think because it enabled him to socialise with the local girls, but I found the whole business alienating. My father (a very good man without a religious cell in his body) did his best to protect me, often telling my mother, of a Sunday morning, the flat lie that I was unwell/very tired/seemed upset, while I was, in fact, listening to Ed 'Stewpot' Stewart hosting *Junior Choice* through an earpiece, with my radio under the pillow.

In Sixth Year at school, I did, for reasons that now escape me, O-Level Religious Studies (there being no Scottish equivalent at the time). I was the only student, and my time was divided between the two school chaplains, the Rev. Dougal (older, one funny eye, very traditional, a tendency to fire and brimstone masking a kind and shy man) and the Rev. MacPherson (young, large, amiable, liberal and inclined to say things like 'The Virgin birth? That's just a story!'). This led to a lot of confused thinking, but that year I ploughed my way through *Good News for Modern Man*, an 'up to date' translation of the Bible. In order to complement my studies I joined the Christian Union. The Christians quite liked having a sceptic in their midst, and I enjoyed singing along to the happy-clappy tunes – 'Silver and gold have I none/But such as I have I give to thee/In the name of Jeeeesusss Christ/Of Nazareth, rise up and walk.'

I did not pause to think about the contradictions or the terrible grammar, for that would have been mean-spirited. There was juice to be drunk and, to be honest, the Christians were a bit of a selection of oddities, even more so than the debaters, so I fitted right in, apart from the small problem of faith. Eventually, touchingly, they presented me with a Bible and a pamphlet called *The Impossibility of Agnosticism*. Well, it seemed plenty possible to me, chaps.

The trajectory of my career in teaching led to my meeting a great many ministers: Wally Shaw; Arnold Brown; Richard Holloway; Jim Purves; Richard Frazer; Alan Copithorne; Humphrey Mildred; Ailsa Maclean. I liked all of these people very much – the first two are written on my heart – and more or less respected them. I just found it increasingly hard to believe that they all thought they were going to live after they died. I think I'll be quite tired by the time I die.

Still, I had to sit through innumerable religious assemblies. This became more and more difficult as I was promoted and thus more visible on the platform, being watched by bored young people. I have a face that is far from inscrutable, and this is a problem in public places, or when one is conducting a job interview and the candidate says something very silly ('I came into teaching because I'm basically very lazy, and I need the bells to keep me going'). And so, when the chaplains of my career pontificated, I had to really think hard about my face, constricting it into seriousness, or worse, laughing if I guessed they were trying to say something funny. I still grimaced sometimes, often when Jesus arrived in the story they were telling. This might, for example, be about two animals in the jungle, say a lion and a mouse – I just always had a sneaking suspicion that, at some point, the mouse was going to gain victory over the lion, or do him a good turn – then Jesus would appear. 'And so it is with us and our relationship with God . . .', Little twists of . . . logic.

Then there was the problem with God and the repetition of truisms, all those times when we were being told to be kind, as if kindness was monopolised by Christians. I was often reminded of a sketch by the Two Ronnies. Barker, dressed as a scoutmaster, has Corbett, dressed as a scout, sitting on his knee (these were different times). Barker says to the young innocent, 'Now, son, always remember, what matters in life is not the things you *say* and *do*, it's the things you *do* and *say*.'

In truth, hundreds of thousands of schoolchildren have to listen to stuff like that every morning, though they are spared the indignity of sitting on the chaplain's knee.

Ailsa was the chaplain at Heriot's throughout my time there, and she was a fine, kind woman. We together visited the parents of a boy who had died and she was great, warm and uncondescending in the face of broken grief. Occasionally, though, she could be exasperated by the failure of the audience in front of her at Assembly to take her homilies quite seriously enough, and thus it was with the Ferrari and the glass of water.

'Good morning, everybody,' Ailsa began, smiling out at the amiable enough audience in front of her, those of them still conscious after my own reading of the five-page School Bulletin.

'I've got a question for you. Would you rather have a Ferrari or a glass of water?'

I confess I guessed where this was going pretty quickly, but I was up there on the platform with Ailsa and Robert Dickson, my deputy. I glanced across at Robert, and said 'A Ferrari?' and he nodded and said 'A Ferrari'.

Throughout the hall, the young people, who, to be fair, had not really been invited to confer, were considering, quite noisily, this problem. A Ferrari or a glass of water – what a conundrum for a Friday morning.

Ailsa continued, with Robert supportively frowning at the Third Year.

'Be quiet please. Well, I expect most of you chose a Ferrari – is that right?'

I, along with those who were playing along, nodded.

'But imagine you were in the middle of the desert. What would you choose then?'

The noise rose instantly. Remember, there were very many clever children at George Heriot's School in 2011. I screwed up my face a bit. There was going to be a message about need, about simplicity. I wondered how God would fit in. Still, I looked at Robert again.

'A Ferrari?' I said.

'A Ferrari,' he responded, smiling his excellent smile, before putting a frown back on to quell the troops.

'Be quiet, please. Be QUIET, please!' Ailsa said, regaining control with a shade of difficulty.

'Now that made you think, didn't it? Because if you were in the desert and the sun was beating down, you would want a glass of water.'

The noise rose instantly. No they wouldn't. They would want the

Ferrari, and it was fairly obvious why. Some of them shook their heads. Others laughed. Robert half rose out of his seat, which would usually be enough, but Ailsa had stirred them.

Ailsa, who always took defeat in her stride, once again asked them to hush, then ran through the rest of her homily. To my shame, I can't remember if God did put in an appearance or not. She did, however, provoke a lively debate for the rest of the day. While I forbade the Debating Society from discussing the motion 'This House would rather have a Ferrari than a glass of water', I did allow myself the pleasure of a conversation at lunchtime with a delegation of S2s, who by this time had compiled a huge list of reasons why, obviously, you would want the Ferrari. E.g.:

- It would provide shade.
- You could trade it with passing Bedouins.
- There might be water in the engine.
- It might conceivably be driveable at least for a bit.
- One glass of water wouldn't last you ten minutes in the desert.
- If you were going to die, at least you would die knowing you had owned a Ferrari.

Etc., etc.

Also 2011

So assemblies were often a bit boring. I confess that and I apologise to all these kids for the millions of girl and boy hours that passed away while we read out notices, praised and blamed, instructed and cajoled, handed out prizes and awards, colours and prefectships, and just blethered. Quite often there were funny things, and occasionally there was some sort of jewel, something that would stick around in your head for some time or for forever.

And so it was with Jamie Steele. Jamie was a 'Foundationer' at Heriot's – his dad had died years before. His dad was Davy Steele, and Davy Steele was a very well-known Scottish folk singer. In 2011 a commemorative concert was held, and his mother, Patsy Seddon, herself a performer, sent me the CD of it. On it, Jamie, then twelve, sings his father's song 'Just One More Chorus', which is a rousing but slightly melancholy song of farewell. Unwisely, I listened to the CD in the car on the way home to Joppa, and placed other drivers in that evening's Edinburgh traffic horror-show in jeopardy by sobbing and sobbing. This wee boy singing his late father's song. So I phoned Patsy and asked her if she thought Jamie would sing the song at Assembly (having, I should say, already managed to sing it very well in front of a huge crowd of strangers) and she agreed. I am not sure by what mechanism she persuaded Jamie, but he arrived in the Hall that morning, polite, thin and pale, with his mother and her clarsach.

I introduced them and they came on the stage. The school pupils were excited and thus noisy, but Patsy struck a chord on her harp and they hushed. Then Jamie sang, in a pure, reedy voice, the song that his late father had left for him to sing:

'Just one more chorus before we depart,
Just one more song we all sing from the heart
The harmonies ring to the words we all know
Just one more song, then we'll go.'

He sang to the School Hall, bound up together in love and awash with tears.

Blanche and Brick: How Times Change

Of course, English teachers talk about sex a lot. This is because they've done English degrees. Academics in English departments talk about sex constantly, or at least they did in the Seventies. I imagine it may be discouraged now, in favour of lengthy discourses on feminism and 'queer theory'. I remember once being in a tutorial at university with a trendy lecturer who read us some short poems by Theodore Roethke, the subject of that week's discussion. Roethke's father was a market gardener on a large scale, and these poems were all about time

121

spent alone in greenhouses as an adolescent, about droopy flowers, 'black hairy roots' and 'pale tendrilous horns'. The tutor, bearded and bejeaned and, let's be honest, quite sexy, said, 'So what are these poems about, then?' Nobody said anything, so he encouraged us to read them again to ourselves. Time passed, and he repeated his question.

'Em, they're about . . . flowers?' ventured a sweet girl.

'Nah,' said Nick loudly. 'They're about wanking!'

From then on, every time my opinion was sought on any text, my first thought was that it might be about wanking, and, to be honest, it often was.

I taught the plays of Tennessee Williams for years. I keep my copy of *A Streetcar Named Desire* in a plastic bag, for it is in bits, written all over. Every time one of my pupils said something clever about it, I wrote it down, and the following year I introduced it into my teaching. To be fair, most often I admitted that someone else had done the thinking. Most often.

This is the advantage of teaching English – every class brings something different and fresh, as they drive down that road for the first time. For many years, of course, I taught only boys, and thus felt obliged to read the part of Blanche DuBois, to avoid any charges of effeminacy being thrown at one of the wannabe Stanley Kowalskis. Years later, one of my pupils wrote about me on the website Friends Reunited – 'Cam Wyllie reading Blanche – no wonder I've spent years in therapy.'

Though I say so myself I think I know a lot about Tennessee Williams. I am glad I never met him, because I think he was probably a self-important man, though he had plenty to brag about, and, given that 'the anti-fag battalions were everywhere on the march' at that time, he was very brave. He died the year after I started teaching his work. I thought nothing of this coincidence, and then Hugh MacDiarmid died when I started teaching him, then Bernard Malamud, then Larkin and then, sadly, George Mackay Brown. Only Pinter survived my curse.

Classes really liked Williams. *Streetcar* and *Cat on a Hot Tin Roof* are basically soap operas – sex, violence, poverty and wealth, inheritance, family tensions, marriage, children, all the tropes of the daytime soap are there.

There were, over the years, patterns of reaction to these plays. At Stewart's Melville in 1984, I broached *A Streetcar Named Desire* for the first time and reached the part where Blanche flirts with the paperboy. Williams is not subtle:

Blanche: You – uh – didn't get wet in the shower?
Young Man: No, ma'am. I stepped inside.
Blanche: In a drug-store? And had a soda?
Young Man: Uh huh
Blanche: Chocolate?
Young Man: No, ma'am. Cherry.
Blanche: Mmmmm!
Young Man: A cherry soda!
Blanche: You make my mouth water!

Unsubtle, yes, but one of the happiest moments of my life was explaining to the director of a great production of this play which starred the distinguished Scottish actress, Vivien Heilbron, that 'cherry' was, of course, an American euphemism for 'virgin'.

Once Blanche had kissed the young man, and he had fled, and we had finished reading the scene, I asked my class of seventeen-year-old boys what they would have done if they had been in that position. One of them was a boy who, throughout his school career, was called 'Flea' for reasons unrevealed to me: handsome, quite tough, quite private.

'I would go back the next day and shag her,' he offered to the class discussion. There was much nodding, though one or two demurred – one obviously gay, and one on the basis that she was 'a slag' and he wouldn't touch her.

Thirty-two years later, when I taught the play for the last time, to a mixed class of S5 pupils at Heriot's, I knew what their response would be, and it didn't much involve going back and shagging her. No, by this time we were in the days of a more enlightened approach to relation-ships between thirty-two-year-old women and seventeen-year-old boys – she was simply a predator, and that was all. Or so the girls said; the woke boys nodded. One or two of the boys grimaced. One felt that maybe they were pondering Flea's idea of a further visit, but they weren't going to admit it.

Then there's *Cat on a Hot Tin Roof.* Spoiler alert – one of the main things that happens in the course of this masterpiece is that Brick, the gorgeous alcoholic former athlete, confesses to Maggie (the 'Cat'), who is his beautiful wife, that, years before, his best friend Skipper had phoned him to tell him that he loved him. Brick, disgusted, hung up, then Skipper effectively killed himself. Brick lives with the guilt. When we had done that bit, I used to ask the class what they would do if their best friend phoned up and told them they loved them.

Well, in 1984, Flea was again in no doubt – 'I'd ask him round. And kick his head in.' Even then that wasn't very acceptable – another wee chap, now a professor, bravely said, 'I'd just ask him round,' to the scorn of his wannabe alpha male classmates. But by 2016, of course, everyone was very, very fluffy about their friends loving them. It was absolutely fine (providing of course it was made clear what their own sexual orientation was). Nobody, thank God, worried any more about their friend being gay or bisexual or trans or pansexual or ambisexual or asexual or perisexual or hexasexual (sorry); and to suggest anything different would be a problem. I liked Flea. I am not sure whether, in that scenario, he would really have kicked his friend's head in. Or, indeed, my own. I'm just pleased that his children wouldn't.

Kids Say the Darndest Things . . .

. . . as Tammy Wynette, of whom I am unnaturally fond, remarked in a song with that title in 1973. This led to a TV show in the Nineties in the US, hosted by that (former) icon of American wholesomeness, Bill Cosby, which featured children saying cute things. They do, though. Sometimes witty, sometimes simply daft, sometimes very profound, and often full of an idealism and a naivety that makes you want to laugh or cry or scream.

So, in my first year of teaching, I was marking an essay on *The*

Merchant of Venice – God, I don't like that play – in which the child wrote 'I imagine Shylock as a small fat man with a Dutch cap on his head.'

*

Later, walking across the playground on a sunny day at Heriot's, I entered the low building where I had myself been taught when I was five. There, just inside the door, a youth lolled on the bench, a clever floppy youth.

'Oliver,' I said, with more levity than irritation, 'why are you here? Get out in the sunshine! You have your health and your youth!'

'And you, sir,' he responded, 'have your health.'

*

Remember when Prince died? April 2016. I heard the news on my way to work. I quite liked his music, but it wasn't like Bowie dying, or Leonard Cohen. Or Mama Cass: I was seventeen when she died, and on a strange holiday visiting the cathedral cities of England. I was in Lincoln and stopped to get a paper, found out she had died and cried in the shop. Anyway, Prince died too. At 8.15 a.m. I was in the playground, and walking up the steps I encountered Hugo, aged seven. He was standing further up the steps, and when we stopped our eye level was the same.

'Did you hear about Prince?' he asked.

'Yes, I did.'

'Did you like Prince?'

'I quite liked him.'

'And he was fifty-eight.'

'Yes, terrible.'

'What age are you?'

I was fifty-nine.

*

Years earlier, but on a similar note, a lovely girl called Carmel left school but returned for a music event. She greeted me with genuine warmth; it is always the case in teaching that absence makes the heart grow fonder – the reputations of retired teachers only get enhanced over time. Pupils, when they leave, often colour great chunks of their school life in rosy hues. Carmel was working in a shoe shop, a fancy one.

'Lovely shoes,' I said, 'but too expensive for me.'

'Come in and try some on. If you like them, I'll get staff discount for you. I'll just say you're my grandfather.'

I was thirty-eight.

*

Two girls sitting at lunch as I drift around. They are due to go on trips shortly. One of them, I ascertain, is going to Yorkshire, the other to Morocco. This latter information surprised me – the Morocco trip involved hiking across the Atlas Mountains, in real heat. I have never really understood the attractions of such a trip, but, hey, each to his or her own. Still, I knew this lassie quite well, and she just didn't strike me as the type to want to camp after a twenty-mile hike in the dust.

'Well,' I said, 'that's quite a demanding trip!'

'Yes,' she said. 'It was a mistake. I got confused between Morocco and Monaco, and when I realised I just felt so silly, I couldn't bring myself to ask for a change . . .'

*

I used to tell prospective parents that the kids liked to come to Heriot's – they liked being at school. The evidence was our absence rates which, even in those increasingly snowflakey times, were really low. Anyway, I was in the Quadrangle one day and two Junior School boys, maybe aged ten, walked past. They were a comical couple – one was very tall and the other very small, so the tall one was leaning over the small one so they could converse.

All I heard was the tall one saying – he was quite a posh boy – 'I was sick all night, but I said to my mum, I'm definitely going to school.' Bless.

*

I am teaching *Death of a Salesman*.

'So, what is a tragedy? How do we know this is a tragedy?'

'Good, in a tragedy someone dies at the end. So we know this is a tragedy because?'

'Good. Because of the title. Willy is going to die. Miller didn't originally want that to be the title, and some time [when I remember] I will tell you what he originally wanted to call it. Are you completely with us, Nathan?'

'Ok. So a tragedy ends with somebody dying. A comedy ends with . . .'

'Yes, laughter, but that happens all the way through. If a tragedy ends with death, a comedy ends with?'

'Good, Martha, life! But more specifically – some of you have done *The Merchant of Venice*. Yeah, I'm not all that keen either . . . but it's a comedy because it ends with?'

Martha again, on a roll.

'Marriage! Excellent. Lots of marriages at the end of *Merchant*, and at the end of all comedies by Shakespeare. So tragedies end with death, and comedies end with marriage, because . . . Well, what happens when you get married?'

Some time elapses.

'Yes, sex. Back then, lots of people actually didn't have sex until they married. I know, it's astonishing! Anyway, why do people have sex? Lots of reasons obviously, pleasure being an important one. But at least some married people, at any one time, are having sex because they want? Yes, Paul?'

'Exercise.'

*

But these shards of comedy aren't the deal, really. There were lots of laughs of course, but there was also all the weight of the world.

I taught a boy called Ian a long time ago. He was a polite and kind boy in my remedial set. I knew that his parents were separated, and I knew that his sister lived with his father, and that he lived with his mother. I had met both parents – a blithesome and happy and confident dad, and a sad mother who seemed so much older and said nothing. I felt for her – her happy husband gone off with a younger woman, with a new baby; her daughter refusing to see her; only her sweet boy to give her comfort.

Ian talked to me frequently after school, about how much he missed his dad, and how much he worried about his mother, whose teacups increasingly smelled like whisky. He wanted to leave her and go and stay with his dad, where there was family, but he felt guilty at the idea of leaving his mother, whose behaviour was erratic. It seemed a load for a twelve-year-old. I said, talk to your father, your doctor, your friend's mum, your uncle in Canada, but I don't think he did. One day he came to say that he had told his mother he was going. Her response was to tell him she was dying of cancer, and that he should stay with her until she died. He didn't think this was true, but what should he do?

How would I know? Sometimes you just felt so useless. And so lucky.

A Plagiarism on Both Your Houses

All the way through my career, I was always really interested in the teaching of creative writing. Very early in my time at Stewart's Melville I taught a boy called Grant who was not an easy boy: tall, skinny, angry, lazy, sharp. I really liked him. He was in a class that contained a number of golden boys – handsome, academically successful, sporty, this was so important of course – and they were really cheerful as well. Grant smoked in school and was depressed. His tie looked like he had been chewing it. His hair was lank and long. But he was very clever and, on good days, very funny, and deep inside he wanted to please. I made his class write lots of poems, and one day he presented me with this:

Blackout

No one comes out to the park
Where normally there's light

A veil of darkness climbs the street,
As day's replaced by night.
The swirling dark encases fog,
To chase a stray dog's feet.
And barking, runs off through the mist,
And up the new-veiled street.
I watch the movement from my door,
To see the fading sky.
The shrinking atmospheric void
Surrenders with a sigh.

Aaah. These moments in teaching are like long cool glasses of water. A lot of him in there, but a little bit of me. When I gave the class back their work (there was another beauty about a clown) I told them how pleased I was, then said that this one, Grant's one, had just knocked the ball completely out the park. Then I made him read it out to them, and, pinkly, he did so. He was so pleased. I was so pleased. At break, I made the other English teachers listen to it. Ah . . . but. His teacher from the previous year, on hearing who had written the poem said, 'He didn't write that. I guarantee it. He's pullin' the wool over your eyes, Mr Wyllie,' and laughed away. I was sure he was wrong, but it chewed at me through a rather dull double period on punctuation or something, and at lunch I sought Grant out before he disappeared shed-wards for his lunchtime No 6.

He was furious. I got the whole lot. It had taken him ages. He thought I believed in him. Did I think he would do that? Then I could fuck right off.

Fortunately this exchange took place in my classroom, though I knew it would have been the same reaction had I attempted a quiet word in the playground. He made to leave, and then I made the mistake of saying that the suspicion had been suggested to me by another teacher. He correctly identified the gentleman concerned. This led to a rather unpleasant confrontation, but, in time, and with some grace, the other teacher apologised and some sense of order was restored.

It has to be said, however, that in the same year I submitted a group of poems about animals to a competition, and was very pleased when one of them, a short descriptive verse about swallows, won a prize. I made a big thing out of it with the class, because the boy who had written it was a wee shy boy of twelve, and I sometimes worried he was a bit out of things. For the poem he got a clap at Assembly, and much praise from me, and then we got a letter saying it had won through to the next stage and was going to be in a book. Even better news! I wrote to his parents to say how pleased I was.

Then he came to see me. He hadn't written it. Not only that, but it was in fact written by Andrew Young, a distinguished Scottish poet and clergyman who, had he still been alive in 1982 when this happened, would have been ninety-seven. Not only that, it was in his big sister's school poetry anthology. I instantly phoned the publisher and told them what had happened; fortunately the book was not yet printed. He was suspended. It was very embarrassing all round.

Every year for twenty years I did the same task with my CSYS, later Advanced Higher, class. We would start by reading an unusual little poem by Hugo Williams called 'Dinner with my Mother' which is a lovely, slight, touching piece, with no rhyme or particular rhythm or indeed, any imagery in it. Some of them loved it, and some of them thought it was nothing at all. But it made a point about the nature of poetry, before they started writing their own. The task was to go away and write a poem about a relative, they handed them in and I read them. Then I took half a dozen of them and mixed them in with half a dozen or so poems by 'proper poets', including the Australian genius Les Murray, Liz Lochhead, Louis MacNeice ('Come back early or never come'), the lyrics to the song 'My Father Always Promised Us' by Judy Collins, and Theodore Roethke's 'My Papa's Waltz' (one of his few poems not about wanking). Obviously, I also put in Larkin's 'This Be the Verse' which suggests 'they fuck you up' – 'they' being your parents. (Often they thought that the Larkin must be by one of the class because 'real' poets would never say 'fuck'.) Then we sat in class for a double period and they discussed which ones they thought were by their peers and which ones were by the actual published poets. This often proved to be my favourite class of the year.

The first year I did it was my first year as Head of English at Heriot's, and Dr Elizabeth Thomson and I took the class away for a creative writing retreat to the school's outdoor education centre at Forest Lodge near Bridge of Orchy. I had envisaged something like a nice youth hostel, but actually the property was, at that time, very run down, and I slept with a piece of plastic sheeting covering a large hole in the ceiling of my freezing room. It also transpired that we couldn't get the hot water to work, which in these days when teenagers shower twice a day – as opposed to my youth where we bathed once a week – caused uproar. Anyway, we worked and we ate and we gave them a glass of wine with their spag bol and we went for a healthy walk. And we did the poetry task.

Now Dr Thomson was a brilliant lassie, and the kids called her 'Doc T'. She and I, in the spirit of mucking in, had also each contributed a poem; hers a clever, rather beautiful poem about her grandparents' house and how she viewed it as she got older. My poem was a tiny thing, which I had written the previous year in the airport of Perth, Australia, waiting to return to Scotland. This is it:

Departure Lounge at Perth International:

Grannies are going home.
Back from their winter in W.A.
To their other winter alone.
Later, wakened from the light sleep
Of their grandchildren's eyes,
They wonder where they are;
In transit, in the skies,
And come so far, so far.

So we are sitting, grubby and cold, in a variety of worn-out seats in Forest Lodge. Nobody knows who has written this poem. To my pleasure about half the kids think it was a 'professional' poem and the others think it was written by one of their number. Doc T explodes with derision.

'It's really not good at all, this,' she says. 'It needs a lot of work.'

'What's wrong with it?' I enquire, quite deliberately leading this young member of the department of which I am the boss towards a deep, dark trench.

'About everything,' she says, and then launches into what I realise is a perfectly fair demolition of my precious little creation.

'I'm sorry, I know that one of you must have written it – but . . .' she concludes.

'No, it was me,' I admit.

Ah, the shade of red she turned, to match her bonny hair. Still, I have never written a poem since, and I won't be sending her this in a hurry.

Over the years that exercise produced a great deal of fairly self-indulgent rambling, some amusing comic verse:

I often want to kill my granny
I'd like to hit her round the head
Or drive a hammer through her brain
Or simply shoot her – dead.
The woman's only four foot ten
And eighty-one years old
But at one time was twenty-three
And five foot one, I'm told.

There was also some pretty conventional 'my brother is a pain but I love him' stuff and a few that were daring to be different.

In among these, there were great beauties. In the first year, a depressed intellectual wrote a poem about his mother which, coincidentally, was also a poem about my mother. It included the line 'Mother has a meat-cleaver in her mouth', something which I used to say to myself on those occasions (increasingly rare, thank God, as I got older), when my mother took something a bit too personally.

I could go on and on about the privilege of reading these words as their first reader. I have kept them all. But this was the best. I'm saying nothing.

Reflection

This is the last of it. Make the most of it
And wring the snaked head. Throttle the slop,
Two week's muck goes down a treat
And splat it on the floor again.
A hallway dance with the dead wood rod.
My magic mop is chomping dust.
Dull morning that it is, nobody's died.
Yet, it's my turn, my turn to clean the porch.
Trust my luck, back and forth, leaning, lurching
Cleaning, and in the background, the commentary
Of the pulsive sea, the beat of my blood.
But back and forth, this is the last of it.
My pills are brown in their bottles,
My cherries fulfilled in their compote,
Six glottal stops are lodged in my throat
Like the impossible lumps, my sick lymph nodes.
This is the last of it: the mop is sopping
And I won't stop. But a puffin goes out
And thuds off the matted sand for the flies.
Back and forth: relent.
I let it dangle dripping, grey bedraggled thing
A dead woman held upside down
Who hangs above the froth
Of what is clean and what is not.
Soon I'll go upstairs and treat the stain:
A cup of tea I spilt the other day.
A waste. A scalding draught
That scorched the tastebuds on my tongue.
But that was the last of it.

The creative writing course became very popular, and one year we had two classes, the other being taught by my friend Sam. She is a wonderful teacher and just a teeny bit competitive. I, on the other hand, have no interest in competition; for me it's really about getting the best out of every child in my care, and if someone else's class does better, well, so be it – I have tried my best. [Yes, yes, I know. The dishonest narrator strikes again. I tell you that wummin wasn't doing better than meeee.]

For our classes we set my other annual task, which was to write a short story where some characteristic of one of the characters was unusual and was central to the story. The stimulus for this was Raymond Carver's extremely short story, *Fat*, which is two and a half pages of understated brilliance which led to great discussions as to what it was about. If you don't know it, read it, and see what you think.

The two classes went off and wrote their stories. Some of them, inevitably, took too much from the stimulus, no matter how hard they tried (*Thin* …), but some of them were exciting and original and thought-through. In my first year at Heriot's a really shy, very clever girl with bright eyes, who was what my great-aunt would have called 'a lovely person', wrote a story about a six-year-old boy in a supermarket, squalling at his mother about not getting sweets, behaving very badly and embarrassing her. They reach the checkout and the kid sees that the checkout boy has a big nose, and laughs and laughs at him. The checkout boy turns very pink – there was a great description of his terrible skin. The hysterical little boy steps outside with his mother, who is now deeply ashamed, turns round for one last look at the big nose and is hit by a car. I liked that.

But this year with Sam we agreed to cross mark; she came and sat in my wee office and we read a few of each other's stories, having provisionally marked them over the weekend (yes, I know lots of people have weekends off, but English teachers have marking).

'They were pretty good, I thought,' she said. 'But this one was FANTASTIC.'

I gave her what I thought was the best of my bunch, and I began to read the story she gave me. After about a minute, I looked at her, screwing up my face.

'It is fantastic.'

She beamed.

'But,' I continued, 'she didn't write it.'

Now, the girl had been extremely unlucky. I do not read that much, which is very poor for an English teacher, I know. Also, I usually do not remember what I read – I have read *Bleak House* three times and loved it, but I will manage a fourth reading if I am spared and will do so not knowing what happens at the end. What should also have been in her favour was that the story was in a collection which had not even been published in the UK at that time. But by an extraordinary piece of chance, however, I had literally read it the week before, having been sent the book from the USA. God, looking down on all of us sinners, was playing a hard game with this lassie. And it mattered – this was Exam Board work, potentially contributing to their grades, and the students had been told how serious plagiarism was.

Sam was furious. She felt she had been had. She was embarrassed about how excited she had been about how good the story was. She intended to disembowel the girl. So we saw her together, Sam pale and almost trembling with rage, and me, I'm sorry to say, quite amused and trying to hide it.

'Alpaca,' I began (this was not her real name), 'we really liked your story.'

'Thank you,' she said, looked wholly happy and entirely unfazed.

I looked at Sam to ensure she was not dismantling the pencil sharpener in search of a blade.

'But we just need to check that you didn't have any help with it, because it is extremely good.'

'Well,' she said, looking at the ground, then looking up, 'I did show it to my mother, who suggested one or two changes.'

She was so convincing I sent her away, knowing that I had to have this American book in front of me before I started again.

The next day she came back.

By this time her goose was a charred mess at the back of the oven. Her first two paragraphs followed the American story word for word. But still I gave her one more chance.

'So, Alpaca, I just wanted to check once more that you were quite sure you alone were responsible for the story.'

She smiled broadly. Yes, she was sure.

'OK,' I said, sighing, for now she would surely be suspended. 'This is the start of your story: "The night was very dark, but Geordie could see the way home because the diamonds of snow brightly glistened for him."'

She beamed.

'And this is the opening sentence of A. J. Aardvark's story, "How Geordie got home": "The night was very dark, but Geordie could see the way home because the diamonds of snow brightly glistened for him." And the next two hundred words of his story are the same as yours.'

She looked at me. She looked at Sam, her teacher, sadly shaking her head. I expected her to cry. She took a deep breath.

'What an extraordinary coincidence,' she said.

What Have We Learned about Sex Today?

In the 1970s, like, I suppose, everyone else, I learned about sex using the heuristic techniques that would one day be fashionable in classrooms teaching other sciences. The Wiki article on heuristic learning includes this relevant sentence: 'Examples that employ heuristics include trial and error, a rule of thumb or an educated guess.'

That just about sums up my approach to sex in 1972, except the thumb was not the part of the body that ruled fifteen-year-old me.

I was a late developer, which was lucky really, because it meant that by the time it became possible for me to contemplate the fact that I could have sex, my mind had at least some inklings of what would be expected of my skinny body. Eventually, at lunchtime on a cold day early in 1975, sometime before my eighteenth birthday, at the top of the Modern Languages turret, I learned a great deal very quickly from a rather more experienced peer. But in fact, at every stage of my nascent gay sex life, trial and error, rule of thumb and educated guesses were my friends. That Easter, in the rather safer and more comfortable surroundings of a bungalow in Corstorphine, when that same boy – who seemed like such a sex master to me – said, 'Do you want to fuck me?' I had very little notion of what he meant. Fortuitously he proved a very adept teacher.

I blame the Reverend Steele, the school chaplain in 1970, who had acquired the pleasingly appropriate nickname of 'Stainless' (this differentiated him from Mr Steel, the Head of Geography, who was 'Rusty'). Stainless had packed us into the school chapel, a beautiful but dimly lit, cavernous and cold classroom, to educate us about sex; though that was not, as I recall, ever a word he used. This supposed sex education lasted through four or five sessions, each one starting with the chaplain's warning that 'any boy who laughs is out the chapel'. I was by this time thirteen. I have very little idea what I thought about sex at that point, but I had picked up bits and pieces from a number of sources.

My parents were eclectic and liberal readers; in my father's case this came from his own parents – a copy of the Marquis de Sade's *Justine* was found under my deceased grandfather's bed. Novels of the Sixties and Seventies had plenty of sex in them, and I had many surreptitious reads through the dirtiest bits of my parents' library. Updike, of course. Harold Robbins enjoyed writing scenes in which large-breasted women admired the huge private parts of their lovers: I remember one, attached to a Mexican bandit, being described as a 'broomstick', which even then seemed a mite fanciful. I benefited in particular from a novel about Eskimos which described both vaginal and anal sex in some detail, and in which, once again, the protagonist appeared to have a massive cock (this time a 'mallet'). I did worry a bit about that.

Then there was what one learned from others and by observation. The swimming pool at Heriot's, which was at that time a single-sex school, had changing cubicles without doors, and these afforded the possibility of fairly detailed study of the anatomy of one's peers changing on the other side of the pool. Of course, as one got older, it became important to achieve this with some subtlety, lest one gain a reputation as a 'poof'. I did not perceive myself as a 'poof' when I was twelve or thirteen, even if my favourite pictures from *Disc and Music Echo* were of a shirtless David Cassidy wearing complicated trousers, or (glory be!) the drummer from Sweet in his pants. My indirect, carefully timed observations of my classmates in states of undress confirmed at least one thing that was a source of relief – none of them was possessed of a broomstick or a mallet.

Then there was home. At no stage did my father sit me down and tell me any version of 'the facts of life'. I do remember one night when I was sitting with my mother and my older brother. We were, as ever, watching the television, but I was also drawing in one of the hard-backed science notebooks my dad brought back from the office, and which I loved. I was ten or eleven. I was a terrible artist, but had drawn a tower, made of various objects.

My mother, casting a critical eye over it, said, 'What's that?'

'It's a tower. I'm going to call it "Erection".'

I didn't realise I was gay but I had created an art gallery in the garden hut – this was the late Sixties, so I called it 'The Wyllie Art Gallery of Love'. The gallery/hut was also used for the attempted manufacture of perfume in an old teapot. 'Erection' was to be hung there. Well hung, I imagine.

My mother looked at my brother, very tall and worldly wise.

'Is he being cheeky, or do you think he doesn't know?'

'Know what?' I enquired, answering her question and causing her to explain, in graphic detail, what an erection was, finishing with, 'It wouldn't be much use if it was soft.' Thank you, mother. Wham, bam, thank you ma'am.

Anyway, that or thereabouts was all I knew of sex when I arrived in the chapel for my first sex education lesson with the Reverend Steele. And it was more or less all I knew about sex six weeks later when the course had reached its . . . climax.

Each lesson was accompanied by a film strip, and – I kid you not – the second one actually was about birds and bees, the first having not dared to stray into the animal world, lest we become inflamed, and having focused entirely on procreation in plants. Eventually, yes, there were diagrams of the male and female private parts. However, the explanation of what was done with them remained unillustrated, focusing very much on the production of babies, and the seriousness of undertaking such a decisive act. There were no questions. I expect

I was in the same boat as all young people then. Sex was presented as a kind of embarrassing ritual, necessary to having kids, and, to be honest, it didn't seem to me to have much to do with the drummer from Sweet in his pants.

Many years later, a friendly librarian presented me with a pair of instructive books. The first, published shortly before the First World War, is *How to Make the Most of Life and Other Talks to Boy Scouts*, a collection of speeches, of which my favourite remains 'How to be Manly' by the Reverend E. W. Shepheard-Walwyn, BA. The other one, published in 1898, is *Confidential Talks with Young Men* by Dr Lyman B. Sperry, from which I used to quote extensively when I taught Psychology a hundred years after its publication. Dr Sperry is admirably graphic in his description of the male reproductive organs, but, perhaps oddly, he does not actually say what they are for, only what they are not for, in a series of chapters called 'Sex, Precocity and Self-Abuse', 'Seminal Emissions', 'Spermatorrhea' (apparently sleeping on your side helps), 'Prostitution', 'Venereal Diseases', and, in a show of glorious irony, 'Quackery and Its Victims'. I have always thought it likely that the Reverend Steele had copies of both books on his shelf, though he did not, praise the Lord, spend time discussing the sheer horrors that awaited anyone who, God forbid, masturbated: weakness, blindness, insanity, even death. Death by wanking.

Years and years later, discussing masturbation with a Sex Ed class of sixteen-year-olds, I commented that it always seemed odd to me that 'wanker' was a term of abuse, having earlier that day stopped an argument in which the insult was thrown. Now, obviously, at some point, it meant 'you are inferior because you can't get sex so you have to wank'; but, hey, most sixteen-year-old boys aren't getting any sex, and wanking, at least in moderation, is a pleasant form of relaxation, so I suggested – as a joke – that 'unwanker' was more appropriately abusive. Such is the power of teaching that they called one another 'unwanker' for months afterwards, so I never ever used that line again.

Before I actually had some sex I therefore had very few pieces of the jigsaw. This was, of course, intensified by the fact I was gay. Apart from the fact that gay people liked to suck cock ('cocksucker') and that bums were involved ('bums to the wall') nothing was ever said.

In 1989 I was talked into teaching some sex education at Daniel Stewart's and Melville College. We showed a series of short films about HIV – there were four of them and we were 'allowed' to show three of them. We showed the one describing what HIV was and how it developed into AIDS; we showed the one which described how you got it; and we showed the one which described what it did to you. However we were not to show the one which showed you how to prevent it, because this involved demonstrating how to put on a condom, and we were of course meant to preach abstinence as a preventative measure for HIV and every other STD (those were described in a number of other lessons). Homosexuality, not long legalised in Scotland, was discussed only in the context of its power to kill you. At no point was it suggested that sex – with a girl, with a boy, with yourself, might be fun, or at least natural. Sex was a weighty responsibility, a burden.

In 2008, at Heriot's I tried again, teaching S5. This was rather different. The course began with an icebreaker in which the single-sex boys' class, in groups, was invited to write down all the names they knew for the male and female private parts, and then there was a plenary session, in which I wrote down all their answers on a big sheet of paper. This was meant to last ten minutes in total, but in their allotted time the groups came up with an astonishingly rich variety of names, and the plenary took the whole period. I did not know, for example, that the labia of a lady could be called a 'camel's toe'. I believed myself quite the expert on other words for a cock, but the class got to around sixty before I began to think they were making them up, and brought an end to that game. Again, I got through the whole course but complained that this time homosexuality was dealt with only in the 'scenarios'. You know the kind of thing: one hypothetical situation about getting pregnant; one about having sex when you're drunk; one about the boy pressuring the girl when she's far from 'ready'; and then, inevitably, one in which your friend tells you that he/she thinks they might be gay (the correct way to respond was with tolerance and sympathy, as if they had told you they had cancer).

I began to feel we were somewhat behind the times when I entertained my friend Heather to lunch. Heather was the Head of Senior School at our major competitor up the road. She was a great pal, who sang from the same hymn sheet as me, a smart, elegant, beautiful woman of much my age, and we lunched together once a term. On this occasion she was late. She had, she said, been taking a Sixth Year Sex Ed class of boys, and discussing ways in which men could pleasure women; there had been, she assured me, a detailed discussion of the necessary manipulation of the clitoris. This had not featured in my own teaching, though I promised her that, had it been expected of me, I would have read up on it.

Nowadays, of course, we are in an entirely different place to that in which wee skinny fifteen-year-old Cameron found himself in 1972. Back then I knew nothing except what an erection was (handily explained by Mum) and how birds reproduced (more clumsily explained by Rev. Steele), and I had clawed my way through ignorant darkness towards some vague light of understanding. But now in the 2020s, and for some years previously, fifteen-year-olds think they know every single little detail of what sex is, because they spend oodles of their time watching porn, or sending pictures of their privates to the kid who sits next to them in Physics or to some stranger in Ecuador. What need for sex education when Timothy can be assured that, later that night, he can watch a man who looks disconcertingly like his grandad performing a full repertoire of sexual acts with identical twins of his gender of choice, this particular clip chosen because said twins resemble the kid who sits next to them in Physics? While Mum and Dad sit below watching *Line of Duty*, Timothy can indulge his fantasy until it dawns on him that his Physics homework remains undone, at which point it may, indeed, be some time around dawn. Sigh.

Pornography is not the least weighty of the things we need to teach about in our Sex Ed classes. We need to explain how studies show so many harms emanating from it, not least in terms of the expectations our young people have these days about what actual sex consists of

– for example sex with actual girls who have actual pubic hair and normal breasts and who themselves don't really know what to do; or with actual boys whose dicks are not broomsticks.

By the time our young people leave school, they need to have been taught various things about sex. Boys and girls need to have been taught what it is that sex consists of between boys and girls, boys and boys and girls and girls, and they all need to have been taught all of it. There need to be two over-riding messages associated with all our teaching about sex – safety and consent. Then, once these two parameters have been established, sex education should be unashamedly accepting of the fact that sex is pleasurable, necessary, healthy and various, and that whatever you want to do – if it is safe and consensual – is fine. Yes, of course, young people need to know about STDs and date rape, but they also need to know about orgasms and lubrication and the many, many things that people find pleasurable. They need to be taught not to be ashamed of their bodies. We need to move away from the myth that young people will somehow 'know' when the time is right for them to have sex, and really concentrate on helping them avoid being pressured into it. We also need to help them with 'relationships', that associated, but not identical, area of study. As a general truth, after thirty years of guidance work, I can honestly say that it's relationships that are hard on young people, much harder than sex, but it's sex that their parents and their teachers seem to fear. It's as if we are all living in about 1950 in a suburban house in a medium-sized American town, and that our teenagers are moving inexorably towards the day when they will meet the 'right' person (who will be of the opposite sex); after a lengthy period of courtship, various stages of sexual behaviour will develop between them (mainly led by the boy and resisted by the girl). It is, outside certain religious circles, accepted that these couples may even live together without being married, but it is expected that their relationship will be monogamous, and will, in time, include children. It is also a relationship which will go on till death. Well, hey, if it happens, God bless, but let's not pretend that it's the only satisfactory way to live your life, otherwise the huge gap in perception between the older and younger generations simply gets wider and wider. Kids already think they know more than adults; in these days of Pornhub and Grindr and Snapchat, sex is not the mystery it was, but we are still teaching about it as if we alone were the experts, when, in truth, no one is ever an expert in this subject area. I've barely scraped a pass at Higher, myself.

On Further Reflection

Boys and Girls

When I went to Heriot's as a child, it was a boys' school, and I didn't think about the lack of girls ever. I liked girls when I met them, and made friends with them easily, in the way that nascent gay teen boys do, but I didn't miss them at school. You don't miss what you don't know. And so it was when I went to teach at DSMC: there weren't any girls, and I didn't miss teaching them. The boys did some things with the girls from the Mary Erskine School up the road – all sorts of things, one imagines – and that was fine, and the girls were lovely and clever and happy, but I didn't miss teaching them any more than I had missed being taught with them. Then I went to Heriot's and it was very, very different. Quickly I wished I had been to a mixed school, and – no matter how much I loved my years at Stew Mel – I came to wonder why anyone sent their boys, or indeed their girls, to a single-sex school. I still wonder that.

Are there legitimate arguments remaining in favour of separate schooling for boys and girls? Let's look at a few, and remember I'm not an educationalist, I'm a teacher; I haven't done any academic research, so everything I say is anecdotal, but hey, life is a long series of anecdotes really.

Firstly, there's the argument which says that 'boys and girls learn differently'. I don't know if that's got any real basis. I think they behave differently and that might affect their learning sometimes. I think they look at teachers differently. Here's an anecdote – this was 1991 and things are a bit different now.

When I arrived at Heriot's as the Head of the English department, I took the top set in S3 and I loved them, but after about three weeks I said to a wise lady that I thought the boys liked me more than the girls, and I wondered if that was because I had only taught boys before.

147

Well, a couple of days later, she came back and said no, her investigations suggested that the girls did really like me, but that sometimes it took time for them to establish relationships with teachers. And the girls were quieter, more conscientious, more organised, more liable to get things right when questioned. They looked at me differently, with a less distracted air; they made more notes; they laughed less, but smiled more. I loved teaching them, they indulged me, they were in lots of respects easier than boys.

One day I was feeling really sick, but I went in anyway – teachers do this – and felt sicker as the day progressed. So when this lovely class appeared for the last two periods of the day, I told them just to sit and read, and answer questions. This was not my style, which more usually involved a kind of mix of personal interaction and stand-up, with occasional vague wisps of scholarship. But I imagine I looked like papyrus, so they more or less did as they were bidden, occasionally looking up to ensure that I had not died.

At the front were two very brilliant, very smiley girls, one shy and the other not. This latter eventually said to me, 'You really don't look well. You should go home. Would you like some paracetamol or something?'

I assented, and off she went to matron, her shy friend with her to open the doors, for she would need to bring a glass of water too, wouldn't she. They went and came back very fast and gave me my pills and my water. I was, of course, astonished. In the past, with Third Year boys, no matter whether they loved me, liked me or loathed me, I could have entered the room with a spear through my head and no-one would have asked if I wanted a paracetamol. But I don't think the fact that girls are more 'emotionally intelligent', or empathic or mature, means that they should be educated separately, because that's life.

Then there's sex, this fabulous nonsensical idea that the studies of young people in mixed schools are constantly undermined by the presence of the opposite sex – a view borne out, I imagine, by research showing that gay children in single-sex schools perform much worse than their straight counterparts? This weird notion takes as a given that the adolescent obsession with sex is tempered by removing the object of that obsession. Actually, if anything the opposite is true, certainly as suggested by my research at Carbisdale Castle, where, for many years, I went with Stew Mel boys and Mary Erskine school-girls, all in S3. This was, for many of them, their first post-pubertal shimmy with the opposite sex, and both sexes went a bit crazy. There seemed to be such an emphasis on sex, you could almost smell their brains burning. Of course, it was all regulated and great fun was had by all, but there was an underlying edge of the dangerous unknown. Whereas when, a decade later, I did the same trip with Heriot's, there was none of that – the boys and girls were used to being with each other. Broadly, the girls had girl friends and the boys had boy friends, but there were lots of exceptions, and they all muddled along nicely. There were fewer dramatic incidents during orienteering, or attempts made (usually by girls) to broach the others' dormitories. The atmosphere was all less heightened and hysterical.

To be fair, there was, when I started at Heriot's, a tendency among certain of the older staff to describe some girls as 'daft about boys'. I responded occasionally at meetings by suggesting that the odd boy was 'daft about girls', just to see what happened. I suspect that showing too much interest in girls was regarded, perhaps perversely, among some of these gnarled veterans of the classroom as being unmanly, whereas I think they thought it funny that less able girls would actually fancy boys. I myself didn't see much sign of daftness by either gender; their feelings were much more likely to manifest themselves as boredom, tolerance, amusement, kindness and scorn, rather than the wide-eyed boy band hysteria I had seen in single-sex environments.

At Heriot's we once took in a clever, rather stylish girl for S5 who, at her admissions interview, said she couldn't stand being at a single-sex school anymore and she wanted to be somewhere where there were boys to talk to. She was clear and confident about this; her kindly, clever father seemed slightly embarrassed, as if his daughter was seeking treatment for sex addiction. Anyway, she came, and about six weeks into term I encountered her and asked how she was getting on. Her enthusiasm for her new school was such that I asked her to come and speak with me and Jo Easton, who ran admissions. She said she thought the mixed environment was more natural and less stressful for the girls. She was pleased to note, for example, that the girls didn't wear much makeup. At her old school, she said, the girls wore lots of makeup 'just in case a boy dropped in'.

Boys and girls are simply good for one another. Boys swear less, wash more and are less homophobic in a mixed school; girls are less inclined to stress and bitch when their friendships go wrong, which can be ghastly beyond words. Boys will often provide emotional solace.

Then there's the argument about academic results. Apparently it is still believed that in the 2020s, some male teachers will favour boys over girls, and will think, if not actually say, 'No dear, stand back and let Butch do this, lest your pretty hair gets set on fire by the big frightening Bunsen burner.' The argument is that the effect of this is to demoralise girls, naturally enough. Except of course, it's bollocks (I've gone for the precise scientific word, you will realise). Girls do better, on average, than boys in S4 and S5 exams; there's generally a bit of evening out in S6, as the boys catch up in terms of maturity, and – sometimes – have to push themselves harder in S6 anyway. As a rule, girls at single-sex schools do better than boys at single-sex schools, and girls at single-sex schools very often do better than the overall results of boys and girls at mixed schools. However – stay with me – if you separate out boys' and girls' results in mixed schools, the girls' results are very often better than those of single-sex girls' schools. Of course, none of this matters, because exam league tables don't matter relative to the personal happiness and fulfilment of the children, but please, please don't use results as an argument about the superiority of single-sex schools.

Finally, schools are meant to be 'microcosms of society', aren't they? Society, last time I looked, had men and women working away together in it, and that seems to work.

Of course, they do fancy each other. A long time ago I was teaching a Second Year class when a new Fifth Year boy was brought in to be introduced. He was an Eastern European scholar called Petr, and, because he hadn't started yet, he wasn't in uniform, but in a shirt and tight blue jeans, as boys from Eastern Europe often like to be. All these scholars were a joy – very clever, conscientious, talented, and he, additionally, was fresh-faced, innocent, blue-eyed and pleasing to the eye.

My class was working on something quietly, but more or less as he stepped into the room a fabulous, kind and daft girl called Alison said 'He's fucking gorgeousss', in a tone of wistful desire. I pretended to ignore this while I established that Petr's English was more or less already perfect, and that he was, you know, a published poet in six languages and an expert zither player and represented his country at volleyball and stuff like that. Then I said, 'I think you should have a tour of the school, Petr. Alison, could you look after Petr?'

The class roared. Alison arose, so purple with embarrassment that she looked like she'd had a stroke, but she was game, so off they went for what turned out to be a long tour, innocent, joyful, natural, fun. It is good to make young people happy.

Drugs

For about thirty years I made a wee recurrent joke in the classroom. If someone – and it was almost always some cheerful, dozy boy – said something weird in answering a question, I would look at him quizzically and say 'drugs?', and generally people would laugh. Sometimes they laughed so loudly that I realised I had inadvertently hit on an actual dopehead. I suppose I thought I was being a teeny bit outrageous, because drugs are the official no-go area in schools. And in homes. They are, in truth, the great divider between parents and their children, and between schools and common sense.

I have never really understood why this is, at least as far as it concerns the use of dope – and for most of my teaching career, the word 'drugs' was more or less a euphemism for the various methods of consuming marijuana. Only in later years was it clear that some young people had decided that sitting in a back bedroom in a circle with a badly made joint, and hoping that the smell wouldn't linger on the curtains, was a mite passé, and turned to pills, including, of course, horse tranquilliser.

I have never got that one – if it tranquillises a horse, what does it do to skinny youths?

Anyway, like more or less everyone who was at university in the Seventies, I smoked a little poor quality weak grass. The first time was in the flat of a clever gay American postgraduate, and it was exactly that situation where your extremely impressive host seems to assume that you have done this before and will want to do it now. I was terrified, but the stuff had absolutely no effect on me at all, possessing not even the hit of the first Embassy Tipped of the day, my favoured fag of the moment. I suppose I then smoked it again four or five times, but it failed to provoke such pleasure that I would ever really have taken the risk of buying some, which might have led to trouble. By that time I was a confirmed young gay man, and it being 1976, I always thought the police were breathing down my neck anyway.

Consider the way in which parents deal with alcohol as opposed to the sheer horror of their reaction to drugs. It is, of course, illegal for young people to drink until they reach the right age – but drinking is apparently thought of as an acceptable rite of passage, something your children have to learn on their way to proper 'adulthood'. Once, very late at night, following the after-the-Christmas-ball staff party in a house near DSMC, I returned, horribly drunk, to the school car park, so I could be driven home by a rather severe and wholly sober female colleague, who was, I am confident, regretting the invitation to car-share home. It was very cold, I was shivering in my tuxedo, slipping in the frost, a light snow was falling in the moonlight, when we realised there was a girl, in full ball regalia, sitting on the ground beside the solitary car left. She was conscious, but utterly pissed, and freezing cold; if it had been darker we might have missed her. She had been sick, and then, I think, more or less dumped by her friends, or her partner at the ball. We drove her home, and made sure she could walk to the door, ring the doorbell, and get inside. She could, of course, have died. Drunk boys and girls whom I knew – lots of excellent kids – have fallen through plate-glass windows, tried to kill themselves, had their stomachs pumped, been arrested for running on top of parked cars, walked on the edges of tall buildings and, of course, vomited endlessly, on the best carpet, in the car, in the fishtank, on their mum. Still, I sometimes think their parents think this is inevitable, as they themselves head to the pub or pour another G and T.

But smoking dope, ye gods. I have great friends whom I got to know when they were parents. They slaved for years working in their hotel to pay the school fees: kind people, generous hosts, funny, real. They were liberal enough parents whose kids had beers and wine long before they really should have. On one occasion, though, the news reached them that we had suspended someone for bringing a tiny morsel of dope to school and then, sigh, showing it to a friend. It was nothing to do with their children directly, but my goodness, what a terrified phone call I had from them. Could it really be true, that there were drugs in the school?

It's all about keeping things in proportion and being realistic. I used to teach Psychology (about which I know only what I was taught in Moray House in 1980) for one period a week to Sixth Year pupils. I did the same set of lectures for about twenty-five years, usually to a group of about seventy or eighty young people. Much of what I 'taught' was populist social psychology, and, very often, I ended up using these slots to test the water on whatever was bothering me professionally at the time, since, let us be honest, 'psychology' covers a lot of ground.

One day, just before this class, we had just asked someone to leave because he had been smoking dope at break. His teacher, a really decent guy with a sense of duty, had – without any pleasure – phoned my friend Robert Dickson, my deputy, my rock, and told him that he thought this boy was stoned. Robert who – I'm just guessing here – does not have even my own tiny history with 'drugs', told me, and then, together, we interviewed the boy, a really quiet, decent, inconspicuous type.

'So,' I said, beginning in my time-honoured fashion, 'do you know why you're here?'

'No idea,' he said and giggled.

'Well, you seem very … cheerful. We just wondered if you had been using anything today that might have made you seem a bit … cheerful.'

For a moment he looked more serious, then smiled broadly. 'Yeah,' he said.

'Have you been smoking dope at break, by any chance?'

'Yeah,' he said, and laughed. 'Sorry, Mr Wyllie. Sorry, Mr Dickson. Sorry.'

Robert intervened. 'Have you got anything on you now that we should know about?'

'Yeah, a bit,' he replied. 'Do you want it?'

Actually, I could probably have smoked it then myself, but – probably just as well – Robert took it; it was in a pretty little leather pouch with a large cannabis leaf on it.

'Nice,' Robert said as he took it. He wasn't being sarcastic or mean – this was a good, quite clever, polite boy who hadn't done a thing wrong before, and we knew where this was, inevitably, headed. Robert just wanted it to be as painless as possible.

We got him out the room for a moment, had a brief conference about what a huge pity this was, and I phoned his dad, who went 'raj' – I think that's the teenage vernacular expression – and asked what was I accusing his son of? This was ridiculous. He would be coming immediately and bringing his legal team.

I suggested that, perhaps, he might just come and talk to his son first, and fortunately he turned up at my office alone, assuring me that his 'legal team' were on call close by. 'Yeah yeah,' I thought.

So Robert, raging parent and I saw the boy. I realised, when he came back into the room, he was – and I confess to being relieved – still well away in a marshy, flowery world.

'Now,' said Dad, 'what is all this about? Mr Wyllie says you have confessed to smoking drugs. At break. Now, is this true?'

'Yeah,' said the boy. 'Sorry, Dad.'

Undaunted, the father rushed to the conventional stage two defence. It is a kind of chess.

'Who made you do this? You are a good boy. Who made you do this?'

The boy looked around blankly.

'Nobody.'

I could tell that Robert was bursting to slap the father about the chops with his son's bag of cannabis, but the trajectory of the conversation was fine, so I was prepared to let Dad do the time-honoured defence dance.

'Well,' he said, searching for the new argument, 'who gave it to you? Did someone plant it on you? Who was it?'

The boy was sadder now, embarrassed by the palpable show of his old man's love for him, moved by his dad's unawareness of how his good son lived his actual life.

'Dad,' he said, 'honestly, I just bought it from my usual guy in the Meadows.'

There was nothing else for any of us to say. The boy, I'm glad to say, had an unconditional university offer to do Business somewhere and could just leave school, so the Dad withdrew him, which was inevitably what he had to do. Robert was sad but resigned, and I was very unhappy with myself. He'd done one wrong thing once, this boy, and that was him out. He hadn't slapped anyone around, or kicked a teacher, or molested someone or taken a small boy's lunch money. He'd just gone out at break and smoked a bit of a joint, and he'd probably done that before and been fine. But he left that day.

A few days later, there I was with his year group. It would have been wrong of me to talk about it directly with them, and they would have thought I was being disingenuous if I had told them how sad it had made me. So I asked them to think about this question: 'In the past week, what proportion of the Sixth Year will have used some form or other of drugs, excluding alcohol and tobacco, or been offered them? No conferring.'

'Right,' I said, after a few minutes. 'I am going to give a figure myself and I want you to comment on it. Seventy per cent.'

Some of them laughed, I thought because they thought I was making a dog's arse of playing at cool.

'Jeremiah,' I said to the excellent school captain, a very clever, very smiling, very Christian boy who would not ever, ever, have used drugs, and who was not called Jeremiah, though he might have been. Despite my heathen status, I think he liked me. He nodded. He was serious.

'I think,' he said, 'that seventy per cent is too low.' He looked at his friends, his year, as they nodded in agreement. 'Way too low,' someone said.

They were lovely kids. Most of them were never in trouble. They went on to be doctors and lawyers and actors and designers and civil servants and nurses, but Jeremiah, who would not have told me a lie, thought that more than seventy per cent of them had used – or at least been offered – drugs in the past week. And we'd just chucked out an otherwise blameless child who – stupidly – had smoked a puff or two too many at 11.00 am.

At Carbisdale, one year, on our annual Third Year outdoor education fest, there was a drugs bust. Lots of years on, the kids from then still talk about it and how badly it was handled. That was me handling it, and, in a sense, it was my fault, though there was no way of seeing how events would, ghastly, ghastly, unfold.

This all happened because some dope brought some dope with him, clearly not fancying a week away abseiling and canoeing and hill-climbing and mountain-biking, without some dangerous and cool relief. It would be hypocritical of me to be too aghast, not because I had a teenage cannabis habit, but because I too would have hated a week doing these things when I was fifteen. Or indeed, fifty-two.

So Weed (not his real name) brought this smidgeon of dope with him; the tiniest morsel, not enough to get his pet hamster stoned, far less himself or any of the three others he shared it with.

It would please me greatly to tell the world (well, the 0.00005 per cent who might read this or be bothered) what actually happened on that and subsequent days, because the issue fomented great discontent among that long-ago year group, who blamed entirely the wrong people for the great mess that happened. I am mindful, though, that lots of kids were upset and had their lives changed, and stirring that up, even in the interests of 'truth', might cause further pain. However, it was, excluding the deaths of children, the worst thing that happened to me in my career, because we ended up seeing several excellent young people leaving.

But their leaving changed the law. Once the cannabis dust had settled, and with the Headmaster's approval, I talked to the Board of Governors about please, please, allowing there to be discretion in future cases like this, and they agreed. A bit too late for Weed, and for his friends, and for the boy with the pretty leather pouch, or indeed for another dopehead boy – a grand boy – who borrowed some of his dad's stash one day and showed it to someone. Their going pained me.

Yes, yes, I know the arguments! Remember I was a school debating coach so I know arguments about everything, at a very superficial level . . . I know the line about one thing leading to another. You know, just like half a pint of lager and lime leads to cirrhosis of the liver, or a good snog leads to a lifetime of chronic STIs. Yes, I know expelling Weed was meant to prevent him heading off on a road of drug dependency, a harder and harder road. Unfortunately, that argument just doesn't work and I doubt anyone really believes it.

But I do remember James T. He was a clever boy, not popular with all his teachers, not a 'good Herioter', but he had interesting, opinionated things to say. I had made his acquaintance repeatedly because of his minor misdemeanours, and he was always funny, fairly honest and grumpy when punished. We shared lots of detentions, James and I; he was, I suppose, worldly, but not nearly as worldly as he thought he was, as it turned out, because just after he left school he got sent away for 'intention to supply cocaine'. His lovely kind parents blamed themselves, each other, the school, but not with any rancour; they were just heartbroken, and needed to know why.

So I visited him in Polmont Prison for young offenders, and I could see what was happening; I could see that his intellect remained undimmed, and his presumption of his own invulnerability was no more challenged by jail than by a school detention. He was a great deal physically fitter; I'm sure he had made friends there but he simply had to have been scared. He looked like a teddy bear, but he was, in truth, just a tiny bit frightening himself, even though I think he liked me. He and another ex-pupil who was naughty but loveable (the first day I met her she said 'Honestly, Mr Wyllie, I was holding the cigarette for a friend' and I knew we would bond) took me out for dinner a couple of years after James T was released. He wasn't really listening to anything, but he was witty and drunk. I decided I wouldn't do that again, but that didn't matter, because he was dead soon after, of a drug overdose, in the toilet of the bookies' at Jock's Lodge. I suppose I don't think that was anybody's fault, really, but his own, and I don't think it happened because, when he was fourteen, he smoked a joint in some leafy Edinburgh park with some older bad boys. I really don't. Still, I think about him lots, and I'm sorry.

Erts

When I was at school, I had two or three great teachers, some good ones, some who were interesting or funny or warm people but couldn't really teach, and some who were shocking in every respect. But a uniformly unsatisfactory area of education for people of my generation was the teaching of what are now known as 'the expressive arts'. In Scottish schools the current definition includes, logically enough, Art, Music and Drama, but PE is also shoved in, there being nowhere else to put it.

In 1969, most teachers of these expressive arts did not actually teach anything. I don't know if Drama teachers existed anywhere else, but there weren't any at Heriot's until about the year 2000, so that was a pleasure I was denied as a schoolboy. I was terrible at Art, but that didn't really matter – all we did, for years and years, was sit and draw. There was no pretence that anyone was going to teach us how to draw; we just sat there and demonstrated whether we could draw or not, and I could not. No one commented on our work or tried to improve it.

On one occasion, when I was about nine, Mr McCheyne, a stout man with a moustache who was the Head of Art, had us drawing pirates, which was a nice change from the vase we had been drawing for several months before. My pirate's head looked like an egg, with two little egg eyes and a mass of hair; there was a thing on his shoulder which could have been a parrot, or a monkey, or a sack of coal. Mr McCheyne sighed, took his pencil, and with a flick of his hand gave the egg a double chin, and the pirate three dimensions. It was extraordinary, but, of course, it was an accidental intervention – no intention of teaching was involved. On another occasion my friend Colin and I were wandering along the Art corridor at lunchtime, avoiding the rough playground. The corridor was lined with reproductions of Old Masters, and we stopped to look at van Eyck's *The Arnolfini Marriage,* which I liked because the husband and wife have heads shaped like eggs. Mr McCheyne emerged from the Art staffroom, asked if we liked the picture, then proceeded to explain its perfect construction, and to fill in some of the historical background, the symbolism etc., etc. I was twelve; it wouldn't have done to ask why we never looked at pictures in Art and instead just drew, badly in my case.

Fifteen years later at Stewart's Melville, I go to fetch a child out of a lesson, and he is in Art. The classroom is in darkness, and the Head of Art, Alex MacMillan, is showing the class some Old Masters and discussing what makes them good. I watch for several minutes as he explains about the golden ratio, about symbolism, about, well, I suppose, Art. He is teaching them, and later seems surprised when I compliment him on his interesting lesson.

In my last two years in Art at school, I barely did anything at all. Instead of working I sat and talked to the teacher, who was young and had long hair and was nicknamed 'Hippy', about pop music, with which I was, by the age of eleven, wholly obsessed. Hippy and I did not have similar tastes, and he tried to educate me away from Motown and the Beach Boys towards more esoteric music – eventually, as I recall, selling me an album by Principal Edwards Magic Theatre for 50p, which, once I had actually heard it, was less of a bargain than I had hoped. He gave me forty-five per cent for Art in S2, which was fair enough given that I had achieved zero per cent.

Music was much the same. The Music department was run by Dr E. E. Smith ('Doc') and Norman Shires ('Horsey'). They had been there forever, to the extent that the words of the school song had been changed from

March on with steady step and true
Like sons of hardy sires

(Yes, really) to

> March on with steady step and true
> Like sons of Horsey Shires

This song, incidentally, was dropped when the school, after about 300 years of only educating boys, took in girls. The first line was 'While gratitude fills every breast . . .' and it was clearly anticipated that the boys would giggle, and thus take away from the decorum of the occasion. This is a pity, for in the views of most aficionados of the school song genre, this song was better than the other song, 'The Merry Month of June', the words of which will remain with me well beyond death.

Doc Smith was ancient, and played the organ. Horsey was a bit younger, I suppose, and was delightful – patient, kind, interested. Neither of them was much interested in anything except singing, and Heriot's had no orchestra but was famous for its choirs, which were, of course, all boys. This was fine with me, for I had a strong treble voice (until I was about fifteen, unfortunately). When I was eight, I had a solo in the annual Usher Hall concert; this was a big deal, involving me singing 'Cuckoo, cuckoo' by myself at the end of the Junior School choir's rendition of *The Cuckoo Song*. Two years later I advanced from this to running onstage and shouting 'Oh, what a good boy am I!' at the end of the Senior Choir's performance of some choral arrangements of nursery rhymes. This, as you can probably guess, confirmed my position as an irritating wee knob-end with every child in the school who was older than me, including my brother, who had, in any case, identified me as such some years before. Even my parents seemed slightly embarrassed by my desperate pleasure in showing off. However, my reputation was improved somewhat when I triumphed in P7 in the Junior School Inter-house Music competition singing a Russian folk song. Horsey Shires had spent hours perfecting my enunciation:

> O'er the snooow my sleigh goes speeeding
> Under neath the frrrostty skai

160

And the horses need no leeeaadding
Thrrrooo the na ite to my love they flaai!
Trrrrottting trrrrottting trrrrottting
Never stopping
Merrrrilly they rrace alung
Sing ing sing ing sing ing
Sleighbells rringing
Thrrrough the na ite to my love they flai!

Pleasingly, another child in the competition sang the same song badly, very faintly, sick with nerves and forgetting the words halfway through (as you can see I have never forgotten the words; I expect, in years to come, to sing it in my old-age facility, counting on the likely immobility and deafness of my audience). I won the prize for the best performance, my House won the cup, and for somewhere approaching an hour I was a hero; in my memory I was carried by cheering peers out of the hall, but I doubt that. This was not a rugby match.

Gym was the worst lesson. Anything sporty, really. Performing well in this was, of course, everything, but no one back then ever told you how to do better. You just failed and failed and failed again: at rugby, of course; cricket; athletics; football (not an official game at school, but I still managed to be dreadful in informal kickarounds). In gym class itself, tiny and skinny, I was wondrously awful, even worse than the fat boys. I just couldn't see the point. In S2 we did circuit training, which at least was better than dodgeball, where I was the last to be picked and, despite my build, the first to be despatched. The circuit consisted of six exercises. On the first day we did each exercise vigorously for two minutes, with a partner counting how many times we achieved the outcome – in, say, push-ups, or getting to the top of the wall-bars. Then the circuit consisted of doing half that number on all six exercises. I was always the first person to finish the circuit, since I couldn't actually do three of the exercises at all. But the PE teachers liked me, and often let me prattle away to them while the rest of the class did the manly things. Mr Hastie let me sell the juice at Goldenacre instead of doing cross-country and that was fun. He also, once, tried to show me how to hold a bat during rounders. Apart from that, no one taught me anything. We just did it.

These days, PE teachers are like evangelical Christians: they are full of joy, and they really believe in what they do. Young PE teachers are a tonic to the soul, laughing, bantering, often very nice to look at, something which cannot in general be said for teachers of many other subjects. Of course, this is because, for anyone who actually likes sport or physical things, being a PE teacher must be a dream job. When you're sixteen and captain of the football team, and very possibly more concerned about your abs than your 'A's' and 'B's', it must seem a very pleasing prospect indeed to get a job that involves spending the day with groups of kids playing games – a healthy mind in a healthy body, after all, even if they, at the end of the day, don't worry too much about the mind bit. And they do actually teach stuff – they cajole, they encourage; once I observed a lesson where the class started by running a circuit of the school playground. The teacher, who didn't know I was there, spent most of her time running alongside the two large, not very fit kids at the back, really praising them for trying and completing the task. Back in my day the fat boys were belted by one old sadist, more or less, I think, for being fat. Maybe, I think, maybe, if someone had tried to teach me, maybe I would have been better at it. But hey, probably not.

I Talk a Lot

I have a very limited range of things I could reasonably say I was good at. Here are things I am not good at: cooking; playing any musical instrument; running marathons or half marathons or indeed at all; DIY, including all forms of decorating except, at a stretch, interior; any sport, except, a long time ago, table tennis (which is, let's be honest, quite homosexual as a sport, even being called ping pong in some quarters, which makes it sound like a sex thing); drawing or painting; games of any sort, but particularly chess and cryptic crosswords and Sudoku (what is that about anyway?); doing things to cars, or any mechanical object in need of mending; listening to lectures; watching most things men like on the telly, particularly golf or cricket or foot-ball or motor racing. I could go on and on.

I lack skills. The only thing I can do well is talk. This, too, is ques-tionable; I think even some of my closest friends – or particularly my closest friends – would say that the quantity often exceeds the quality; but I cling hard to talking, conversing, public-speaking, explaining – to these things as proof of some skill on my part.

Anyway, given this 'talent' for talking in public or private – the former something so many people regard with horror but which I have always loved – the only logical activities for me to do at school were public-speaking and debating. The latter was much more com-bative and dangerous, but even so, in my career I trained and watched countless public-speaking teams, ranging from the sublime (a boy, now a judge – of court cases, not public-speaking competitions – giving a talk called 'Is Transubstantiation Cannibalism?') to the ridiculous (a stolid girl from a doomed school talking about her collection of bottles, with visual aids, culminating in her drawing from under the table, with a flourish, 'my favourite bottle, which was given to me by my father' which was the exact shape of an enormous blue cock). So I debated at school, happily but not very well.

When I went to Edinburgh University, I debated, again not bril-liantly, but well enough to become the President of Debates. In these days before social media and 400 TV channels, students actually came and watched debates, and politicians, knowing this, were keener to oblige when invited to speak. Thus I met, for example, Sir Keith Joseph (mad), Jeremy Thorpe (oily), Roy Hattersley (charming), Lord Longford (also mad) and the Duke of Edinburgh, whose capacity to work a room was a lesson in itself. I met the Chair of the English Collective of Prostitutes, who was gorgeous, and also suffered a post-debate dinner with the Society for the Protection of the Unborn Child, where pictures of aborted foetuses were passed round during the starter and a medical practitioner was assaulted.

It was only natural, then, that without much argument I was allowed to take over the Debating Society at Stewart's Melville, and when I went to Heriot's I restored the almost defunct society I had previously headed up as a schoolboy. And this is how it was for thirty-seven years, in which time both schools had, let's not be modest, considerable success in competitive debating. I was even the national coach for Scotland, which enabled me to travel to New Zealand and Bermuda and Cardiff (where we were lodged in a nurses' home where the nurses caroused all night) and to make a fairly feeble attempt at coaching young people who were, by modest estimates, three times cleverer than me. It could be a humbling experience. Having graduated from coach to judge, I once watched a fifteen-year-old Argentinian boy speak for eight minutes on the motion 'This House Believes that the Advertising of Pharmaceutical Products Should be Banned'. It was an issue that I didn't even know was an issue – did you know that advertising medicines isn't allowed in some countries? Anyway, he was great, and afterwards I complimented him, remarking how hard it must be to do something like that in your second language. It turned out he had an Italian mum and a French dad, and English was his fourth language. My Spanish extends to 'May I have a glass of white wine, por favor?' and that's about it.

I was, to be honest, not a great coach at school or national level, but I had a capacity for recognising talent in this arcane endeavour, and I got away with it by smiling and waving at them as they sat waiting to speak. Quite often, not always, debaters were a bit peculiar, the intellectual weedy kids who liked to talk, and I would like to think that some of them found some solace in what may not always have been very easy adolescences in the safe place of the 'debating chamber' (in lots of Scottish schools a big classroom at the end of the hall with the seats cleared, bless those teachers).

Like Noah. Noah came to us for a year from Pittsburgh, though he stayed for two. His parents were academics and his mum had a visiting professorship at the University of Edinburgh. I liked them all immediately, but there was no denying that Noah was, for the population of George Heriot's School, unusual. He was twelve but looked about thirty-five, with his voice broken and actual facial hair. He was clever, funny and excitable, a musical prodigy, but he spoke very slowly indeed. In the early days of the autumn term he gravitated towards adults, not I think because the other S1s were unpleasant to him, but because there was a lack of mutual understanding. This eventually passed, partly due to the common language of football, which Noah understood he had to learn. Often as I walked to lunch he would come to say hello, which was fine, except each sentence contained many words and was spoken very slowly. So he came to Debating, where his uniqueness was always tolerated and eventually loved.

He spoke in a wee public-speaking competition – the kind of thing I have spent 6,809 hours of my life watching and judging, always horrified by the prospect but, eventually, often moved by the work that goes into these speeches on 'My Gran', 'Should we test beauty products on animals?' and 'A Holiday to Remember' (I don't remember them now). Sometimes there is a gem, and so was it with Noah, who elected to speak on 'Pickles'. He was supposed to speak for no more than four minutes, but as the ten-minute mark approached and I moved towards ringing a bell to stop him, I found I couldn't. Everyone – the little debaters, the older debaters giving up their afternoon to watch the kids, the staff – gazed with wonder on this pickle lover, this pickle expert, and exploded with applause when he finished his pickle talk at fourteen minutes and change. The Chairman of the Society then sourced little pickle badges (from Heinz, I still have one) and the debaters wore them as badges of lunacy. An older boy presented a pickle Christmas decoration which became a trophy for something or other. Do not underestimate the importance of these little things in a child's life; trying to win that pickle pin could give a nervous wee girl some focus in what might be a confusing world.

For innumerable Friday afternoons I chaired meetings of the Debating Society in both schools, and I watched hundreds of debates, with generations of strange little talky boys and quieter, better-prepared, bright-eyed girls talking about everything – Scottish Independence, Europe, privacy, homosexuality, military service, feminism, prisons, punishment, trade unions, China, space travel, socialism, religion . . .

There were many Fridays, especially as I got older, when I could have seen debating far enough, and yet, even on those wet days in January when I forced myself up the stone staircase to the excited chatter and energy of forty or fifty 'debaters', I knew it would cheer me. Older clever kids lounging on desks at the back, watching the younger ones bashing out speeches and, by and large, taking them seriously, in the way that they themselves had been taken seriously by older boys and girls now gone to university. And sometimes, very occasionally, young people demonstrating such brilliance of thought that it made you remember why you were there, in that room, the hush only broken by some wee boy eating crisps and by one voice giving a speech thought up the previous night between their Chemistry homework and Snapchat. It was a little home for these young people, as much as the rugby pitch or the orchestra rehearsal, a place they could breathe their particular breaths, and it was not without hope.

The Debating Society was more or less left to its own devices. At Stewart's Melville, in the late Eighties, it became a focus for a spirit of rebellion, and the very clever boys who ran it made it very popular and a little bit dangerous. It was a good thing nobody leaked the details, because some of the things they said might have got them, and, of course, me, into trouble. Things about how the school was, at that time, being run, points often made through vivid and extended analogies with . . . the Vatican, for example. These were, of course, Friday afternoons long before the phrase 'pupil voice' was ever uttered. The Principal, Patrick Tobin, who was in many respects a genial fellow, but who had strong views largely informed by his religion, disliked the whole notion of school debating, because he saw it as a mechanism for teaching young people how to lie. He did deign to appear in a packed debate, on the motion 'This House Would Cease Teaching Religious Education', a subject democratically chosen by a committee on which the Principal did not have many friends. In the debate, which was recorded on video, Patrick said, in opposing the motion, 'Because, gentlemen, why do we educate young men? We educate them to prepare them for death.' He actually said that, and I knew it was time for me to go and teach elsewhere. Otherwise I might have stayed at Stewart's Melville forever.

The apotheosis of Patrick's dislike of debating took place in 1990, when it was decided to send a Scottish team to the then fledgling

World School Debating Championships, and the team selected consisted of three very clever, witty boys from DSMC. The championship was in Winnipeg in Canada, and the team was coached by my friend Brian Gorman. In these days, of course, the only means of getting information about anything going on in Canada was by phone, so all night I lay awake, knowing that my boys were up against Australia in the final, waiting to hear the result. At about 4 am Brian phoned to say they had won, and I cried briefly before going to sleep for a few hours. Driving to school I heard their victory reported on the news; when I arrived there were parents in the car park waiting to congratulate me. In the staffroom a colleague, a clever, cynical man, stood up when I went in.

'It's amazing. Just amazing,' he said. 'What an astonishing thing for the school. Imagine – some Heads get to say that their team has won in the city, or in the region, or once in a blue moon something national, but the world, my goodness!'

Patrick was a bit other-worldly, so I felt it best to check he actually knew this had happened – it was, after all, fresh news, even if, by this time, it had been on the telly. So I went along to his office where he reassured me he was aware and that he was pleased.

As I made my way to register my House group, I was accosted by Benji, a small, clever S1 boy, an enthusiastic debater, who was incandescent with excitement.

'I bet the Principal doesn't even mention it at Assembly,' he said.

'I think he's got to, Benj,' I said. 'They are the world champions.'

Assembly began. Drone, drone, drone. A hymn which, as usual, remained largely unsung. A prayer which, as usual, simply led to a mass shutting of eyes. Then Patrick spoke.

'This,' he began, 'has been the most extraordinary weekend for the school.'

I relaxed. Benji was wrong.

Patrick smiled. 'The First XV lost to Merchiston Castle.'

Through the hall, while Patrick maundered on about the rugby team's loss, there were widespread disbelieving giggles, little explosions. The noise rose, and I worried that someone would get shouted at, when at last he said: 'That's not all. Our debaters won the World Championships. Very well done to them. That is the end of Assembly.'

We rose, all of us skinny talky types, once again shown our place in the world of real men, real believers in the twin towers of faith and sport. Sigh.

*

At Heriot's life was gentler, and latter-day educational theory encouraged freedom of speech. Up to a point.

In late 2013, a rapt crowd of eleven to eighteen-year-olds was listening to a debate on the motion 'This House Believes Feminism Has Gone Too Far'. Yes, I know, not very woke, but I guess the committee thought it might lead to some good-natured banter. The motion was proposed by two jolly, clever, extremely fogeyish chaps, aged seventeen or fifty-eight or so. The opposition was led by Sophie, a small woman of crystalline intelligence, who was simply furious by the time she stood up to speak. Banter, I fear, was not on her mind. After a minute or so of her completely fair but body-piercing rant, the door at the back of the classroom opened and Mr Hector, the then Headmaster, appeared. He was just about to retire and, being a good soul, was doing the rounds of clubs and societies. The room was crowded; nobody saw him except me. Sophie, red of face and utterly in charge said, 'So, ladies and gentlemen, I suppose Mr Fogey thinks I am his inferior because I have a VAGINA and he does not!' Two P7 boys literally fell off their perch in astonishment and pandemonium ensued. Now, Alistair Hector was a cheerful, kind, busy man, and he hadn't been at the Debating Society much. I would just like to reassure him that, in fifty years of debating, man and boy, local, national or international, that was the only time I ever heard anyone screaming the word 'vagina'. Good chap, he never mentioned it. I think Patrick possibly would have.

Thrashings

Miss Middleton belted me. She didn't like me to begin with. Having taught my brother who was tall, neat, clever, studious and handsome, she found that I did not fit the bill of her expectations, being tiny, yappy, immature. I was sweet, but sweet was not to her taste – gall, wormwood, ear of bat, viscera of innocents being more on the menu.

I was nine and John was my friend. He was open, warm, sporty, bright and always looking for the next laugh, which suited my clownish temperament. Miss Middleton liked John and so, one morning, we got to carry the milk crate back to the janitor. Forty little bottles, recently emptied of their warm milk, back in their reinforced wire crate, John on one handle and me on the other. Giddy with glee at the responsibility, we bounced out of the classroom door and started down the concrete stairs a bit too fast, me ahead, and John lost his grip. The crate bashed off the stairs and the bottles, like synchronised swimmers, leapt joyfully into the air, some of them back into the crate, some of them onto the stairs beside us, and two or three bouncing through the gaps in the banister and falling, falling, falling two storeys down to the Music department in the basement, where they noisily smashed. It was, I suppose, my fault, but the inquest was brief anyway. John was rightly exonerated and I was belted, twice on each hand. I cried. Obviously.

I was never belted again. I came close. In P7 – well, I won't go into details, but I poured Dettol on a rival bean plant – Mr Galloway threatened to belt me and whichever rogue was my fellow conspirator. Bean-growing competitions were about fair play and he was a sportsman. Tall, athletic and genuinely angry.

He took a small piece of chalk and placed it on a desk in front of him. Then he took out his belt and raised it.

'Is there any reason,' he said, raising the belt up high and glaring at us, 'why I shouldn't do this to you?'

Then he whammed the belt down very hard, missed the chalk and the desk and struck his own manly thigh – I used to say he hit his balls but I don't think that actually happened. Anyway the moment had gone and he retired to his desk.

I began teaching just at the time when hitting children in order to encourage them to be good went out of fashion. Many older teachers regretted this, but I didn't. While my mother had a fairly well-practised slapping technique (well, what's a woman to do if a boy won't eat his egg custard, blaagh), my father only spanked my brother once and then, according to my mother, swore he would never hit his children again. In this I was like him, I think, and I would have made a terrible hash of belting anyway.

In one of my unsuccessful job interviews a well-meaning school governor asked me what my 'disciplinary style' was. I could not, in truth, look him in the eye and say 'Firm but fair', because even I am not that practised a fibber. I was never firm, though I aspired to be fair. I could have said something with more truth like 'Vacillating and partial', but I probably said that I didn't have a set style, which was at least true.

When I spoke to young teachers or teaching students about discipline, I always said they should be true to their own characters and not pretend. I loved my friend and colleague Robert Dickson who was, for many, many years my right-hand man, and left hand, and both my legs, and I respected him – as did thousands of young people – because he actually was firm but fair, scary but with a sense of humour, the police genes of his parents well established and effective. There were 'lines in the sand' that the young person was ill-advised to cross. But I was not him. In the classroom I depended always on the young people wanting to hear what I said. I was often funny. I talked about all sorts of things, some of them occasionally actually mildly relevant to the course I was teaching. When I was a young teacher I often went home with a metallic taste in my mouth and pondered the day's humiliations, but I'm glad I only rarely pretended to be tough, because it never ended well. On one occasion when a class got out of hand, my disciplinary tactic was to say, 'Please stop doing this or I think I'm going to cry.' It worked, and I used the line for years afterwards, even as a Head, when some decent child was lying because they were afraid.

It is about noon on a hot day in 1983 at Daniel Stewart's and Melville College and the Second Year exams are happening. It is the end of period 4 and, with two other colleagues, I am invigilating the Religious Education exam. God knows why there was a Religious Education exam; it is one of His divinest mysteries. Should I be wrong and Heaven actually exists, during my brief interview I will be asking St Paul why there was a Second Year Religious Education exam at Daniel Stewart's and Melville College; but at that moment, back then, I could only do my bit to keep these 100 boys quiet. There was another forty minutes to go and, since none of them – apart from the one who is now, no doubt, Moderator of the Church of Scotland – gave a tinker's curse about the RE exam, they had 'finished' the exam and were showing their creativity by making planes out of the exam paper. My two colleagues and I knew that it was IMPERATIVE that not one of these planes flew. 'Check your work,' we said. 'I think you may have missed something out,' we said, with a vague air of threat. 'This is RE,' I wanted to say. 'God is watching you.'

Then the bell rang, and, when no one appeared to relieve them, these two yellow-bellied colleagues claimed they had to teach the next lesson and withdrew. And still no one came. Just me, twenty-six-years old, about eight stone, bespectacled, in my cheap suit. And the Second Year en bloc, the pubic male as one large mass. Please someone come, please come, please come . . .

The noise grew. A plane flew. Another. More noise. The Hall was adjacent to the Principal's office. Stately, I rose to the occasion. Literally, I got on the stage.

'BE QUIET!' I roared. 'THERE ARE STILL PEOPLE WORK-ING!' (The future Moderator ploughed on to q. 143, which concerned the place of circumcision of John the Baptist.) 'IF ANYONE, ANYONE TALKS OR IF I SEE ANOTHER PAPER AEROPLANE, NO ONE IN THIS HALL WILL BE GOING FOR LUNCH!'

Silence.

Lunch, lunch, inspirational, Cameron! Boys like lunch, they do! Got them there. Don't smile, don't smile. You've done well.

Relaxing, I took a step back to survey my wondrous empire, suffused with butch joy, and in so doing caused the large portable blackboard on its easel, there to display the timings of exams, to collapse on my head. These things happen, said the Deputy Principal as he took control of the rioting, these things happen. He didn't say 'to silly young poofs', but I felt it in his tone.

Teacherz

I love teachers. I love it when I meet someone and they are a teacher. I used to love it when some young person, in a careers interview, told me that they wanted to be a teacher, and I loved it more if and when they became one. Hell, even the money's not that bad these days.

I used to look forward to days of interviewing teachers, particularly in some subjects, because, let's be honest, a Drama teacher and a Physics teacher are as different as trans models and coal miners. A day spent interviewing Art teachers was a lovely day, where you looked at the beautiful stuff their pupils had created, and sometimes – if you were lucky – at their own work, while all the time wishing that you could match your socks and your tie like that. They made their own clothes and made their own jewellery and smelled nice. I once had a day where I interviewed artists in the morning and teachers of Computer Science in the afternoon. Clever though these latter blighters are, they don't generally make their own clothes and they don't smell at all. And I can tell you, a biologist and a chemist and a physicist are very different to each other, and treat each other with a certain degree of amused suspicion. Suffice to say, lots of kids just do Biology. I think Biology is easier for most young people to understand, but it may also be because I have never met a nasty biologist; there is warmth among the worm dissections.

So I love teachers, but it has to be said there are some crap ones. When I was a schoolboy, there were lots of crap ones, but we didn't really notice. Still, I think that's why so many people in my generation talk about their love of one teacher and one subject – maybe that teacher was really good, or maybe he or she was the competent teacher among a shower of bored and fractious and stupid people who were just looking for easy power, long holidays and the myth of respect. In 1980, when I started teaching, there were still some crap teachers in the building. When I moved to Heriot's in 1991, oh yes, there was still a wedge of crapness in the staffroom, often accompanied by a supreme self-confidence, an intellectual arrogance, and, of course, plain laziness, amid all the greatness, all the professionalism and all the love of the others.

172

But, my goodness, things are so much better now. When I went to Moray House I was accompanied by a whole lot of English graduates who, in their heart of hearts, really wanted to be doing something else, mainly being famous, but who got into teacher training because it was easy to do so. In the Nineties I helped select graduates for teacher training – people who wanted to be English teachers – and it was always encouraging to see such clever, varied, interesting people coming forward. By 2021, entry to teaching was extremely competitive, but it was an easy ride relative to actually getting a permanent job; so, inevitably, the quality of what was going on in schools got higher, regardless of the myth-making perpetrated from behind misty rose-tinted specs of an older generation who loved their teachers because they were 'characters' – even if they didn't actually learn very much from them. 'Old Fatty Saunders – used to take his wooden leg off in class – eventually ended up in jail . . .' So the crapness quotient has fallen away, and our young people get the benefit.

Of course, lovely teachers have always been themselves to blame for much of this problem. It's hard to work in the close proximity that teachers do, in tight, often very small departmental groups of a few people, celebrating birthdays and Christmas, and births and marriages, and commiserating on deaths and failures, then actually to be able to stand back and say 'I'm sorry, John. Thank you for the barbecue last week, and the present for wee Pauline, but actually I have to say that your review suggests you're a crap teacher. In fact, I should have said this years ago, you've always been a crap teacher.' You need to remember that teaching in a secondary school is a very personal profession, where your work isn't scrutinised very much except by the adolescents in front of you, who, let's be frank, don't necessarily know what a good teacher is, and who are very forgiving anyway. You shut that classroom door and you are in charge. Parents often allow their children to suffer crap teachers; I doubt if they would be so happy with a crap brain surgeon or a crap lawyer or even a crap man repairing their washing machine.

This collegiality in the teaching profession, this capacity to care about your colleagues and watch their backs, can go to really extreme lengths, and does so at the expense of the poor bairns sitting in front of Mrs Rubbish or Dr Silly.

When I started working there was a teacher in the school whom I shall call Edmund. He was essentially a poor soul, a sad, obese old man, who lived by himself in the same house he had been born in, surrounded, I was told, by piles of books and ancient magazines. He wore stained suits and whiffed a bit, and he stood in the staffroom at break and talked loudly at you about opera – he was a bit deaf – until some kind colleague came and rescued you, usually on the pretext that some fictional child was at the door with homework or a sore head and had asked for you, which enabled you to escape out the door. It was said that Edmund, years before, had been stick-thin and a brilliant teacher, and, at times, there were glimpses of a powerful intellect as he maundered on about Wagner, while you watched his ill-fitting false teeth dance around in his mouth. Occasionally, when he was angry in class, which was, inevitably, often, his teeth would fall out. It was claimed by many that they had fallen out through the open door of a speeding bus once on a school trip, while he was talking through the bus microphone, no doubt standing at the front, in the days before Elf and Safty. The old Deputy Headmaster, a fine Aberdonian, made it his daily business to visit Edmund's classroom, and usually ended up taking some boy away to his study for a talking to about kindness and respect, for the boys were not kind to Edmund. Mind you, there were hardly any of them there to begin with, because hardly anyone did his subject at exam level and, if they did, they almost universally failed. Everyone said that he must retire sometime and, years after I started working, he did; his retirement speech went on for forty-five minutes before the Principal stepped in to lead the applause.

I could give other examples. Take those teachers who were simply horrible to all young people: there was one mathematician whom I used to compare to a vet who had only gone into the profession for the pleasure of putting animals down. He too was a clever man, but he was bitter and weird and spoke to nearly everyone sarcastically. Or others who simply could not cope disciplinarily. And others who were absent all the time because they were stressed by the job but would not give it up. Or others who were so boring children fell asleep in their classes. Maybe there would be, say, four or five at any one time in a staff of a hundred. But some very unlucky young people might have been taught by two or three of them in the same academic year and consequently did badly, and because they did badly they maybe didn't get into the course they wanted to do. Parents would complain and complain about these few individual colleagues, but nothing was done, at least not back then. United we all uneasily stood. These few individuals might as well have been operating on their pupils' brains blindfold, with a rusty screwdriver in one hand and a bottle of vodka in the other. If teaching is ever to be regarded with real public esteem again in Scotland, as it once was, it has to be possible to make incompetent teachers exit, and exit swiftly, no matter how 'nice' they are to other staff, or how sorry we feel for them. It all simply matters too much. As the poet said, 'The hand that rules the classroom, rocks the world.'

On Being Gay

I realised I was gay when I was fifteen. I should have known earlier, because everyone at school kept telling me I was a poof.

When I was eighteen and went to university I immediately met several young gay men who were very comfortable with their sexual orientation and this helped me, though, truth to tell, I was never particularly anguished about it. I did not relish the painful evening that I came out to my parents, but it was not the tasting menu of recrimination, prejudice and bitterness that some young men and women face. The next day, having telephoned my brother, who, being a worldly chap and living in London was entirely supportive to me, they went to see the family doctor. He kindly explained to them that in these enlightened days of 1976 the NHS would not 'treat' someone who was homosexual – though he offered them counselling, which I thought very funny – and then, as an afterthought, suggested it was not a good idea for me to teach. Hmm.

There is much I could say about being gay back then, and someday

I will. But for now let's remember that Scotland, nowadays seemingly so progressive, did not legalise homosexual acts between consenting men aged twenty-one in private places until 1980, thirteen years after England, and 1980 was coincidentally the year that I started teaching. The year before, when I probably committed a hundred illegal acts, I was at Moray House, training to be an English teacher. Two men whom I knew to be gay, one very camp and the other very 'political', started that course but did not finish it. The former did not cope with teaching practice; the latter just disappeared, but rumours went about that he had been asked, or told, to go.

So I had a career of thirty-eight-years' duration, and all that time I was a practising gay man; indeed I practised so much I must have been nearly perfect. At the start of my career nobody knew for a fact I was gay; by the end I suppose almost everyone did. I took my partner with me to plays and concerts; we dined with the Governors and with other heads. In discussing my own life in class, which I did all the time, I mentioned him often. Once, when I was about forty-five, around 2002, I was involved in a session with Sixth Year students, preparing them for university. One of the scenarios involved finding out that your new roommate was gay. Would this matter to you? Starting a plenary discussion about it, I said, 'How many of you know someone pretty well who is gay?' Immediately about a third of them raised their hands, then a few more, and then there was a buzz of noise, and they all put their hands up and laughed a lot. I was very amused and very pleased.

Recently I read an academic article which, amid a great deal of verbiage and reference to research, posited this question: 'Should gay teachers in schools actively tell their pupils they are gay?' We have come so far. Still, even if it means nascently gay children would have definite role models, I don't think I like the idea of a new teacher arriving to take S2 Physics and starting by proclaiming their sexual orientation, whether they are gay or straight or anything else. I was once talking to a boy called George, when he was about fourteen. He was clever, unruly, sparky, tense, brittle. I was being nice.

'George,' I said, 'I'm not unsympathetic. I think you are very like me when I was your age.'

George exploded into room-shaking sobs, clearly horrified that he was going to grow up to be me (which, incidentally, he certainly did not do).

Also, maybe if I had said 'I'm Mr Wyllie. I'm gay,' then, as well as being sacked, I might have driven lots of young men to say 'That's it. I must try harder to be straight. Perhaps if I find the right girl . . .' echoing what, of course, their granny would tell them when they came out anyway.

But also – as the dentist numbs your mouth, or the consultant starts the colonoscopy, or the butcher prepares your pork belly, do you really want them detailing their sexual preferences? I do get the point, but teachers have a job to do, plus there's all the fun for the kids of guessing. I do not believe, for a single instant, that young people default to the view that their teacher is straight unless it is proven otherwise; to be honest, more likely the opposite.

I do not think it mattered to my career that I was gay; that was probably luck. It may well have been because I remained in the same school for twenty-seven years, and knowing someone is a great defence against prejudice, which is, in essence, mainly just a specialised form of ignorance. When I was fifty, I was head-hunted for the headship of a major Scottish school; I declined to go for interview, because I thought the school was, at that time, a nest of scorpions, even if I did like the pictures of the fancy house I would have had. Today, I almost wish I had, so that on that evening when the candidates were invited, with their spouses, to dine with the Governors, I might have taken along Mr F; my guess is that after that they would have found a myriad of ways of saying no, but I might be wrong.

At Heriot's, however, when I became the Principal on a permanent basis in 2015, the Governors, all of them together, asked me questions. The most interesting one was posed by a kindly old gent, a gently witty, warm individual, someone who was, I was fairly sure, on side with the Wyllie cause.

'Cameron,' he said, 'if you were us, why wouldn't you appoint yourself?'

Well, there were so many reasons, of which I gave three. My second reason was that I wasn't religious, and I thought some people might find that a problem; my third was that I was not personally interested in sport, though I was very supportive of it educationally (this latter was probably the most difficult pill for them to swallow).

But I thought it fair to start by saying, 'Well, you all know that I am not a traditional family man . . .' I know, I should have been braver, but they all knew anyway.

The Chairman, a decent, loyal man, glanced accusingly at his fellow governors – 'Well, that doesn't matter! This is 2015!' and thus the deal was sealed.

On Parents

I Know My Knee

In my managerial days I interviewed a whole host of prospective teachers, young and old. Many of them worked in state schools, and I always asked them what they thought the differences would be between the two sectors. Often they responded by answering the opposite question – what would be the same? 'Well, learners are the same in all schools' – anyone who used the word 'learner' was, of course, immediately off my shortlist anyway. The best answers, as far as I was concerned, would demonstrate an understanding of two things – firstly, that private schools insisted on a big extra-curricular contribution from their staff; and secondly, since most private schools are selective, the chances are there would be a disproportionate number of academic kids. But often they said neither of these things; mostly they said, 'Well, I expect the parents can be difficult.'

I never truly understood that, and for me, it really wasn't true. In thirty-seven years I dealt with three or four truly terrible parents, and, looking back now, I can feel sorry for them. One of them was actually mentally ill and a terrible thing had happened to her (I can say this now – at the time of my 'chat' with her I actually thought she was going to kill me) and the other bampots had been driven to derangement by their fears for their variously unwell or violent or wholly spoilt children; this state of affairs often, in my experience, being worsened by religious faith.

Most of the time, the parents I knew and worked with were a joy – kind, grateful, interested, wary, and in love with their children, but willing to accept that I and my colleagues were professionals who liked, rather than adored, their offspring. This meant there was a greater possibility (greater than zero) that we could deal with them with a vague degree of objectivity, informed by our learning, our experience, and our knowledge of all the young people we had ever taught. But after dealing with all these parents, thousands of them, some of whom became real friends, and a few, I suppose, who must still spit blood at the thought of me, my conclusion's pretty simple. Most parents love their children with an intensity beyond any other love – a wonderful thing, which nurtures and supports the young people; and so by contrast, when your mum and dad do fuck you up, it's really terrible. Whatever happens, these parental emotions render every parent an unreliable witness as to the character, work ethic, intelligence, charm and talent of their child. And, actually, even as to their looks. I remember a dad saying to me how very pleased he was that both his sons were very handsome; and one of them really was, but the other looked like Fred the Flour Man.

I inwardly sighed whenever a parent said 'Now, I know I'm his/ her mother/father, Mr Wyllie, but I can stand back and look at him/ her ...' No, you can't, I wanted to shout, you can't stand back, you're standing right on top of them, and I guess you always will be. In an ideal world, a parent/pupil/teacher meeting should consist of a conversation between the teacher and the pupil, with the parents only being allowed to say 'Thank you' at the end. Sigh, that will never happen.

I sometimes wonder what would happen if parents treated teachers the same way as patients treat doctors. Let's imagine for a moment that the way in which the general population viewed teachers and the way in which it viewed doctors were reversed. On one side of town a mother is at a Parents' Night at school talking to the teacher (doctor):

Parent: How is Jimmy getting on with his Chemistry, teacher?

Teacher: Well, his overall mark is a bit down on the last time I saw you, and to be honest, I think the symptoms are fairly typical of an attack of adolescent laziness. His exam pressure has gone down, which can be a good sign in some young people, but I'm afraid Jimmy's has gone down to virtually zero, so sometimes in class it appears that he is unconscious. So I'm going to give you a prescription for a set of past papers, and I want him to do one of these twice a week till May. He should try and do them before meals, because his mind will be a bit sharper. He also needs to get more rest, so please ensure that he's asleep by ten every night and maybe get him to cut back a bit on his use of social media. Exercise would help.

Parent: Thank you, teacher. Sorry to take up so much of your time, because I know how busy you are.

Meanwhile, on the other side of town, a man is having a medical examination with his doctor (teacher):

Doctor: So what's the problem, Mr McDonald? How can I help you?

Patient: Well, it's my knee. It's a bit painful in the mornings and sore when I walk.

Doctor: Let me just have a look [examines knee]. Yes, I think it's probably the beginnings of osteoarthritis, so we need to look at . . .

Patient: I don't think so. I don't think that's the problem at all. What you forget is that it's my knee, and I've known my knee all my life and I can stand back and look at my knee and I can tell you it's a very good knee, very hard-working and well-behaved, not like other people's knees. No, the problem's not with my knee, the problem's with you – I think there's bad chemistry between my knee and you. My knee had Dr Smith last year and really liked her – I think she really understood my knee, and now you're saying my knee's got osteoarthritis and you're throwing away its dream of being an Olympic sprinter . . .

Parental objectivity will particularly never happen when a child is in trouble. A very long time ago I heard from a Head about some repeated instances of stealing which had taken place in their PE department. Every week, during an all-girls class, things were being removed from the 'valuables box' which was kept in a little ante-room, and which was just a cardboard box, because nothing had ever been stolen from it in the living memory of the staff. Now, however, it appeared that, in the course of three or four weekly lessons in a row, some person or persons unknown went into this ante-room and snatched something from the box – a watch, a bracelet, a £5 note. So the school fitted a hidden security camera, and, sure enough, the next week, there it was – one of the girls sneaking into the little room, presumably while the others were caught up in the volleyball or whatever, or while she was supposed to be at the toilet, or when she was 'off PE' (many, many young people, girls particularly, skive PE, for all sorts of reasons, serious and trivial, mainly to do with changing or their hair). She then went into the box, took something and, as she left, stared straight up at the hidden camera, which caught her anxious face perfectly. During the next period, this was discovered, she was sent for, and admitted – poor girl – that she was stealing compulsively, not just in PE, but whenever she could.

The Head was sympathetic as the girl sat and cried, but, of course, she had to be suspended, so the Head called a parent, and was connected to her father. Given that the girl had admitted it, and the key thing was to deal with her distress, the Head forebore to mention the camera, even when the father flatly denied that it was remotely possible that his wee lassie could do such a thing. He shouted about false accusation/entrapment/bullying/litigation/assassination/torture etc., etc., while the Head sighed and listened, then said he needed to come and collect his weeping daughter, because she was going home for several days. He was coming, he said, with his lawyer. (As an aside, let me proudly say that in all my years, I never actually met any parent's lawyer, though I did once meet a very suspicious 'aunt' who accompanied a bristling mother, and who took copious notes.) So dad and lawyer (several hundred an hour, I imagine) appeared, and the Head failed to calm him down. The girl had, the father averred without talking to his daughter, been bullied into confessing, either by the criminal themselves, or, more likely, by the staff.

Now, teachers don't like being accused of bullying children. I have known one or two instances where a teacher bullied a child, but this nice old lady wasn't a bully, and she was very sorry for the wee girl, so eventually she explained the history and admitted that a security camera had been involved. Then she showed dad, and lawyer, the footage – the girl, there, in black and white, stealing, then looking straight into the camera. The Head said to me that the father had immediately started to sob, and then, as soon as he was able to control himself said, 'That child is not my daughter,' with such vehemence that, for a moment, this charming and wise and highly experienced Head thought that she had actually summoned the wrong parent, or that he was, horrified, disowning her. But no, it was just a daddy putting up a final line of defence of his little girl.

As a consequence I developed a rule when I was a Head. If a child is in trouble and it is necessary to communicate with the parent, try, where possible, to contact the parent of the same gender. Dads expect their boys to be a bit bad, but for mums they represent everything their husband once was, without the bad bits. Mums understand girls better and are tougher with them as a result; dads are just crazy about their little girls. I realise I am generalising wildly.

Barbara Kingsolver, the American novelist, wrote 'Kids don't stay with you if you do it right. It's the one job where, the better you are, the more surely you won't be needed in the long run.' This is genius. In some distilled form, it should be the first rule of parenting, to make your children independent people, while understanding that that doesn't mean you can't continue to love them. Making your children independent does of course involve some discipline. I have a skewed view of this, because discipline was a bit radical when I was a child, and mainly involved my mother slapping us. Once that had happened it was over, but it wasn't good – much of my childhood involved being very careful not to antagonise my mother, on the basis that if she was happy, I was happy (this is the only thing, apart from sexual orientation, I have in common with Elton John). My dad never laid a hand on us, and distressing him was, thus, much worse. The fashion for hitting your kids has fortunately largely passed, due to parenting styles and legislation and child protection – one boy reported his father to me for slapping his calf when he wouldn't get out of bed. I was, of course, much more sympathetic to the father than the boy. Had it been clear I was deliberately making myself late for school my mother would have kneecapped me.

I once – gloriously – was talking to a very lazy, personable boy about his indolence and lack of progress. He was much more interested in being charming to girls and smoking than in Physics (just imagine!). There he was, smiling sweetly at me and agreeing, meaninglessly, to change his fickle ways, while his mother, who worked eighty hours a week to pay the school fees, sat beside him. Eventually she noticed him becoming distracted, apologised for this, then set about him, bashing away with her handbag. This led to a greater degree of concentration in the latter half of this pastoral interview. You will be astonished to learn that I did not inform the Child Protection Officer.

Maths and Beauty

At one time I did a lot of careers work; I wouldn't get to do it now, because I laboured under the misapprehension that young people might be interested in the teacher's own view of what they might do at university or for a living – stating your view's not allowed these days. Very often I would have talked to the student first, then saw them with their parent(s). I would say very early on to the parents, 'What do you want them to do?' in the hope that they would say 'We want him to do whatever will make him/her happy,' because that gave me the latitude to help the young person break the news. I knew well that, quite often, when a parent said that, they actually meant 'We want whatever will make her/him happy, and we know that what will make him/her happy will involve studying Medical Science at Cambridge, then specialising in Oncology, while at the same time continuing to pursue his/her ambition of winning an Olympic medal, meeting a nice girl/boy, marrying in a major Edinburgh church and having three intelligent and attractive children. This is what will make him/her happy.' When the parent said this, their child, wary, loving, alienated, alert, but who really wanted to study Music and become a jazz trumpeter, would often nod in agreement, to my despair.

I was, for example, sitting in my office one day with a boy I knew very well, and who had previously confessed to me that he did not want to study Business, which is what his dad wanted him to do, but to study Theology and become a teacher of Religious Education. In front of me, he very nervously explained all this, and his lovely mum said, 'Why didn't you say – that's fine,' until interrupted by her husband who said, 'Do you think I paid all that money in fees for you to become a TEACHER?!' of course bringing back memories of my own parents' reaction when I came out as a prospective dominie. The mother pointed out that maybe that was a mite rude, given that I was a teacher, but the father did not relent. Another time, a very good girl who wanted to do Catering rather than Law (Lord, give me cakes rather than conveyancing) came back years later to invite me and her Head of Year for afternoon tea in the hotel whose tea shop she was managing. She wouldn't have been a happy lawyer, but she loved her work.

We can't blame parents for this. Of course, they aspire for their children to 'do better' than them. They are often ashamed of what they do themselves, even when their hard work or craftsmanship or kindness to others has been an inspiration to their children. I love doctors and I even quite like some lawyers, but God, not everybody has to be one.

Of course, there are exceptions – those parents who cheerfully support their children in doing whatever they want to do. On one occasion I was interviewing a lovely, cheerful girl, going into her final year, with her mother in attendance.

'So, we've chosen your subjects for next year. What is all this leading to?'

'I want to study Beauty,' she said. I was pleased. I understand Beauty. I think that spending your life making people more beautiful is a splendid aspiration. I wish someone would take the time to make me more beautiful, using whatever instruments and potions and skills are necessary. I beamed at her.

'Well, Mr Wyllie,' said the mother. And I thought, ah here we go. Mother will want her to do a degree in International Business with Legal Studies. I shall fight and fight for Beauty. But I was wrong.

'If she wants to do Beauty, that's fine with me, providing she understands how much work it is.'

'Yes, indeed,' I said, knowing no more about Beauty than the average forty-year-old homosexual, which is, obviously, quite a lot.

'I mean, I'm a beautician myself,' the mother continued, 'and if I had known how hard it would be to become a beautician, I would just have studied Medicine.'

I wanted to hug her.

It was not always this easy, and for some reason Maths was often at the root of the problem. The teaching of Maths is, of course, vital for our economic well-being, but no matter how hard Maths teachers (a rich and varied bunch) try, some young people are never going to get Higher Maths. At one lunchtime a mother came to see me to plead for her son to be allowed to continue the Higher Maths course. He had got twenty-seven per cent in the prelim; because I am positive and soft I had allowed him to continue to the 'end of course test'. It had been agreed that if he got forty per cent or more in that he could sit the final exam. He got nineteen per cent. He was doing three other Highers and might pass them all with a good wind behind him.

Now, Heriot's does get really good exam results. It is very easy to say that schools stop people from doing exams in order to keep up their exam results so that they do well in the league tables. Actually, schools stop young people from continuing to do courses because they can see disaster ahead. It is done not to destroy their dreams but to stop them walking off a cliff. Of course, all this would be clear if instead of telling the general public what any given school's Higher pass rate was, they instead told you how many Highers, on average, each child went home with. That is actually the key statistic. It's easier to pass an exam if you're only doing one.

But Mrs Wardrobe was having none of this. She was a fine person, who had come in her lunch hour, wearing the uniform of her profession. She worked hard to support her son, and clearly did not comprehend the depths of his idleness. She would work extra shifts in order to finance yet more Maths tuition. Anyway, it was wrong to prevent young people from following their dreams. He would be an engineer. The school could not stop him. All parents thought it was wrong. They all knew that Teddy was a good boy. He had many friends. She changed tack – this was a personal thing – she claimed I did not like Teddy. My antipathy to Teddy was odd, because she on the other hand thought that I was an inspirational person, noted for my kindness. Her daughter – whom I had taught – thought this. Teddy did not agree. In other words, she vacillated between bitter derision and obsequious pleading.

My face was screwed up in despair when she started to cry. And she really, really cried, letting out years of frustration. Why, she might reasonably have been thinking, did Teddy not work hard like his sister? Why was he so rude to her when she loved him and loved him and loved him?

Let's be frank, I was very soft. The Head of Maths was very understanding when I told her that Teddy would, contrary to everything I had previously said, be sitting Higher Maths. She sighed and looked at me with the affection given to the useless manager by those who would not choose to be in that position.

So Teddy sat Higher Maths. No doubt hundreds of pounds were spent on tutoring provided by enthusiastic undergraduates. And he passed, just. But he failed the other three exams spectacularly. I did not respond to his mother's triumphant letter. He is not, I suspect, an engineer. But he is loved by his mother.

Grit

'Resilience' has been a buzzword in education for a long time now. We are told that our children need to be resilient, they need to be more independent, they need to mature sooner. After all, their grandparents lived in holes in the ground and started in the mine when they were twelve, owned nothing till they were thirty-five, paying rent even for the pot they pissed in. Today, young people have everything, they are 'snowflakes'; one private school in England proudly advertises that it gives lessons in 'grit'.

I can imagine the Grit curriculum, and I expect parents thoroughly approve. It will involve abseiling down the sides of cliffs being watched over by teams of experienced instructors; there will, in practice, be absolutely no risk at all. It will involve plenty of team games to encourage camaraderie, teamwork and common goals – though what this has to do with encouraging individual self-discipline I don't know. I very much approve of the Duke of Edinburgh's Award, but I always thought it odd that a child who had just spent three nights on a remote moor with only three equally inexperienced friends – and occasionally some hooch – wasn't allowed to get the bus home from the school at the end of the expedition.

Heriot's was right in the middle of town, easily accessible by bus and train, but the school's life was constantly fraught by issues to do with parents in their cars. It was the same at Stewart's Melville, where I once approached a parent who was triple-parked beside the bus stop in Queensferry Road, his car almost on the other side of the road. I suggested he move and he told me to fuck off. I took his registration number and Robin Morgan reported him to the police. He also suggested that his son could fuck off from the school (his exact words). But still these parents, who so loved rugby and parachute jumps and wild swimming wouldn't let their kids get a bus home.

When I started as a wee boy at Heriot's primary school we lived in Kirkliston, which is now a small town with an Edinburgh postcode, but was then a wee village, quite rural really, eight miles from the big city. My father was then the Works chemist of the malt products factory in the village, which meant he worked a short walk from our home. We didn't, at that time, have a car and, for reasons I do not fully understand, but had, I fear, quite a lot to do with laziness, my mother had nothing to do with the business of getting us to school. She liked her bed and she liked her own company, the house cleared of my father till lunchtime, and of yappy me and my brother till after school. But we had, of course, to get there.

The morning was not a problem. Jimmy, my tall and clever brother, was four years older and was thus, at nine, deemed perfectly competent to escort me to school. So my father woke us at 6.30 every morning and at 7.10 we got on the bus, which took half an hour to shuffle along a road which no longer exists, past the airport and into Edinburgh. There, on my father's instruction – he accompanied us on the occasion of my first day – we disembarked at the West End and walked to Heriot's by a route involving passing through the old Caledonian Station, along King's Stables Road, past the headquarters of the South of Scotland Electricity Board (where my mother would eventually work), into the Grassmarket, then up the 100 steps of the Vennel to the school. Yes, I realise the detail will mean nothing to many of you, but it was quite a walk. And it was completely unnecessary. If we had stayed on the bus for two more stops we could have walked up the Mound – a walk of about half the distance. I was an adult before I realised that; my father, in fact, always had a terrible sense of direction – which I inherited – specialising in 'short cuts' that were no such thing, more like 'long additions'. For the first seven years of school I took the long addition to Heriot's. Jimmy, of course, did not actually accompany me . . . I scuttled along in his wake, often letting him march completely out of sight, while I was dillying and dallying and talking to strangers whom I knew not to talk to. One man, who worked in said Electricity Board, took to carrying my bag for me. I quite liked that. I was five. He was a nice old man – no doubt today he would be arrested.

In the afternoon, a different arrangement had to be made, because the littlest kids got out an hour before the big boys. So my father took a long lunch break – having started work half an hour earlier, while my mother had a nap – and came to get me. He then trained me in easy stages to get home by myself, starting by meeting me at the classroom door, then at the school gate, then at the top of the Vennel, then the bottom, then (big step) letting me get on the number 2 bus from the Grassmarket to the Haymarket, then (bigger step) letting me cross the busy road when I got off that bus to meet him at the SMT bus stop for the long bus journey (38 to Stirling, or 39 to Callendar or Crieff) home. After another week of this, I did the whole journey by myself, so that by the time I reached my sixth birthday I was going home alone, and I did that every day for years. It was, Edinburgh geographers will have realised, another ridiculous route. I suppose there is no question but that the social services would be involved now, but in fact there were a number of us teeny private school kids who got that Stirling bus, with no parents in sight. I remember a girl called Fenella (this in the days when most kids were given normal names; even Cameron was quite exotic) who went to Lansdowne House, a tiny girls' school now long defunct. She was probably a year older, but seemed fabulously sophisticated. She was a farmer's daughter and her sophistication showed itself, I recall, in her school cape, which I quietly coveted, but she never let me try on.

People were kind to small children on buses. My grandmother travelled on this service regularly and knew all the bus conductresses very well, they to a woman subscribing to the myth that she was a 'wonderful woman'. At the Maybury roundabout, halfway home, large numbers of older women would board, having finished their day at Reed's Paper Products. I would rise and give one of them my seat, and, over time, they rewarded me – biscuits, sweeties, wee cartons of juice and, of course, paper products. Various people befriended me. There was a curious man who worked at the airport who gave me an extravagantly illustrated book on Russia, in Russian, which also contained some fairly graphic pictures of a whaling expedition, on part of which, I think, he claimed to have been. There was another man who lived in the village and who my father told me to keep away from, whom I talked to a lot because it is not actually possible for a seven-year-old to prevent a paying adult passenger from sitting beside him. I did not think it likely he would tell my father. I think these people protected me. We live in different times now – it's scarcely possible to comprehend the idea that anyone would initiate a conversation, just a day to day chat, with such a little boy sitting by himself on any bus.

Otherwise I read, or did my homework, such as it was. For a little while in P2 I worked on a coaster we were embroidering in hand-work – a wheel of cardboard we embellished with knitting wool. As a special treat I was allowed to take this artefact away from the class, in order to carry on with its decoration.

Sometimes, when I think about all the kids I taught, who at fourteen or fifteen were still picked up at the school gate by a harassed parent, I think of me, six, embroidering on the number 38 bus to Stirling.

Forgive Your Parents

In a hotel in Jordan many years ago I was in the company of some expats, who were in part celebrating the arrival of the first child of one of their number. The pictures were admired, and then my friend Joyce, a thoughtful and kind woman, said, 'So what do you wish for your child?' Well, the answer to that was pretty obvious (good health, happiness, to live in a world without fear of war or poverty etc.), but that led on to a more interesting conversation about what characteristics we would most like our children to have. I have no children, and the real answer would be 'to be not very like me', but, mischievously, I suggested good looks. That was decried by everybody as very superficial (incidentally, it's probably a good bet – we all know lots of very good-looking people who, despite the lack of other qualities, have done well) and the qualities I should have mentioned came thick and fast – kindness, honesty, integrity, humility. All very well, in theory, I thought, so then I suggested intelligence. And that was the end of the conversation, because no one really truly likes to talk about that.

A long time ago, in a school in the faraway north (of Edinburgh) I had, in my Higher English class, a boy whom I will call Ross – this is also what his parents called him.

Ross was new into the school, and was a great boy – kind, cheerful, hard-working. He became popular very quickly because he liked everybody, was quite sporty, wholly lacked conceit and was polite and respectful to teachers in a very genuine way. He did his Higher English prelim and failed it and then we had Parents' Night.

I am sitting with his mum and dad, and this was in the days before (heaven forfend) the students themselves came to meetings, a step which, of course, made them infinitely more useful. I begin by praising Ross as a model of decency, maturity and hard work. I suggested that they should be really proud of Ross, and, shyly, these nice people concurred. And then I carried on: 'So, as regards the prelim, he demonstrated real progress and I think, if his attitude to work carries on like it is, he will pass at the end of the day.'

'Why did he fail the prelim?' asked his mother.

'He finds some of the work quite difficult,' I said, 'but he's trying very hard.'

'Maybe he needs to do some extra work?' she responded.

'He already is. He volunteered. He's just done a big interpretation which I've marked [aarrgghh] and given him back. He sat down with me on Wednesday and we went over it.'

'Do you think,' the mother paused, '. . . it might be your teaching?'

Ross's father stirred in his seat. 'No, he really likes Mr Wyllie,' he said pointedly to his wife.

'Well, what is it, then?' she carried on.

Her last remark had irked me, I admit, but she had boxed me into the corner anyway.

'He's just not very clever,' I said; then watched, horrified, as Ross's mother burst into tears.

All this chat about kindness and honesty is great, but a great number of parents would sacrifice them for the brains of Hannibal Lecter.

Every parenting experience is unique, and there is a weight of responsibility on both sides – parent and child – to get it right. The balance, of course, shifts. The world of a three-year-old is entirely dominated by mum and dad, or mum, or dad, or granny, or big brother, or whoever is doing the parenting. As the child ages and becomes more independent, that domination, no matter how hard a parent may try, lessens, until, at last, responsibility often shifts entirely to the child, to provide their aged parent with companionship, or accommodation, or money or love – to be there with them at the doctor's, so they can tell them what has just happened, or try to. To suffer with them as they age and falter. Some parents, and some children, get this gloriously right; some muddle along, some fail and some never try in the first place. Some of this is written in the history of our parents' own parenting, and their parents before them. Often, when young people were complaining about their parents, I wanted to ask them what their grandparents were like, and to say, 'Remember, your parents were brought up by these people' – Larkin's 'fools in old style hats and coats'.

Along the path of this change in responsibility, most of us move from wholehearted acceptance of parents, as if they held us in the hollow of their hands, to a more measured view, though it can, of course, never be objective. It is a trope of adolescence that we shun, even despise, our parents, for the brief hormonal passage of puberty. Once, in a distant galaxy, thousands of years ago, I was at a Parents' Night – this was also in the days when the young people themselves were not present, leaving the parents to translate the message for them, in the car travelling home on murky November Edinburgh nights, a translation often less positive than what had actually been said. At this one, a rather older pair of parents, academics, old-fashioned, listened to me waxing eloquent about their only son – his intelligence, his creativity, his generosity of spirit, his sense of humour, his maturity – 'He often hangs about at the end of the school day for a chat ...'

Mother looked at father, who smiled bitterly. 'Mr Wyllie,' he said, 'he hasn't spoken to us for six months, and we don't know why. Might you ask him, during one of your wee chats?'

The fault, of course, lies on both sides. Every fifteen-year-old should be compelled to sit, one day, under formal exam conditions, and write an essay called 'How I Feel Today' in which they outline their hopes and dreams, their fears and worries, and, in particular, in which they talk about their parents, knowing that their words will only ever be read by themselves. These documents would be then taken and sealed, and left unread until that young person is themselves the parent of a fifteen-year-old, their eldest child, when they will be returned to that parent for reading – say, twenty-five or thirty years later. That would, I think, in many cases, lead to a greater level of understanding of their own child's fragile adolescent experience. I don't know what I would have said myself, when I was fifteen – a small, late developer, obsessed with pop music, with a growing sense of being gay, cheerful, talkative, quite bright, with a father who unequivocally loved and supported his two very different sons, and a mother whose own troubled childhood led to an emotional volatility which meant I crept about on the thinnest of ice, trying constantly to please. Would I have known all that then? Or would I just have written a lengthy appreciation of the Beach Boys and Mama Cass and how pleased I was with my first pair of jeans from Top Man?

In essence, we have to forgive our parents, unless we are in the very small minority of people who have been so badly used in childhood that we can never do so. When we are about forty, we need to say something serious to our parents, and they to us. We need to recognise that parenting is astonishingly difficult, completely unpredictable, a witches' brew of genetics and experience and love and raw instinct. And we need to accept that rough patches happen and we need to be kind about that, so that our own children will reward us with kindness in their turn.

Thank You

Rooky: Why I Became a Teacher

At the end of August 1969, I went into First Year at Heriot's and on the first day of that new school year, when Edinburgh was lost in the Festival, I went to Room 65 for English and met Mr Caw, Jimmy Caw, who had been at Heriot's for a bit. Like all the staff he had a nickname, and his was Rooky. Rooky Caw.

For five years my favourite part of the school day was English in Room 65. Not only that, but Jimmy Caw introduced me to debating, and encouraged me to realise that the fact I could talk and talk and talk whenever allowed might, in certain restricted circumstances, actually be a good thing.

That first day of senior school, squeaky me was sitting next to giggling David Small, in the top class for English, excited as March hares, half-bonkers with the thrill of it all – the new kids, the new rooms, the new teachers; and here was Rooky – small, grey suited, plumpish, with odd curly white hair round a bald spot. I suppose I thought he was about sixty; he must have been, say, thirty-eight. He started to learn our names, our surnames of course, for that, in those days, is what we were called by. When I told him my name, he pleased me by not immediately mentioning my brother, which other teachers had done. Then he gave us some rules: our homework had to be on time, it was no excuse to say the dog had attacked it – he would look to see if it was dog-eared. I laughed.

'Why are you laughing, Wyllie?' he said.

'You made a joke.'

'What kind of joke?'

'Was it a pun?'

'Good.'

He smiled. And that was that. He was my favourite teacher, and English was my favourite subject.

In those days at Heriot's you had the same English teacher for five years. When I became the Head of English I immediately stopped that practice; it was fine if you had a good teacher, but not so fine if you didn't. Five years of Mr Caw was, however, bliss, even if he did occasionally forget that he had taught us something and teach us it again. And again. And again. The origin of the word 'pedigree'; the four humours, which have led to some rich words – phlegmatic, sanguine, bilious and . . . something else. Any time someone coughed repeatedly in class he would say, 'Ah, Duncan, one clean shirt will see you out,' in a couthy Scots voice. But he taught us Keats and Hardy and Shakespeare and Ted Hughes, and sometimes in the decades ahead I heard his voice coming through my mouth as I repeated his wisdom, and if someone coughed I did the clean shirt line.

He had us talking a lot, not something that happened in most class-rooms in the Seventies – well, at least, not as part of the lesson. Once we had to do an oral book review and, with just a hint of modernity, he had us working in pairs. David and I, being awash with pretension, did Freud's *The Interpretation of Dreams* which I, at least, did not remotely understand. This enabled us to hint towards lots of areas not generally covered in the S2 curriculum, the impressiveness of all this supposedly mature chat being perhaps slightly undermined by David's inability to stop laughing. At the conclusion of our review, we invited our class-mates to tell us about their dreams. One brave soul said that he dreamt a lot about fish. David stroked his chin and said, 'Hmm. A blocked-up sexual urge.' Another said that he often dreamt he was a Roman soldier. I looked at David – 'A blocked-up sexual urge, Professor?' Then Rooky brought the lesson to an end, but he didn't complain.

He could be a little daring. The Literary and Dramatic Society of George Heriot's School, the 'Lit', met on Friday evenings from 7 pm to 8.30 pm. For those of us who were not sportsmen this was a joy, being mainly an opportunity to talk a lot. And dress up; I had a little cravat that I liked to wear which my grandma gave me and my father did not like. The big event of the Lit calendar was the Burns Supper, held in the School Refectory with the gurls of James Gillespie's High School for Gurls. Some of these gurls, when I was older, and went to parties, became real friends. I think they liked me because, having no sexual interest, I did not distinguish among them in terms of looks or weight; in any case, my voice broke late and I was a harmless wee blond chatterer, confident and guileless, and their mothers liked me. The Headmistress of Gillespie's at that time was Miss McIvor. I recall her as a small woman of great antiquity, who, for the occasion of this Burns Supper, wore a white fur coat into which she more or less disappeared. It was very cold in January in the Refectory.

Mr Caw did the 'Toast to the Lassies', and turning to the lady headmistress said:

'Ae fond kiss; and then we sever

Lest we get caught by Miss McIvor.'

Everyone thought this was glorious except, of course, the lady herself.

Rooky never belted us; indeed, he never raised his voice. We just wanted to listen and learn and please him. He was our celebrity, and for a while in S1, we made up songs about him in the playground to the tunes of current hits. Once, another teacher, a kind and funny man, walked into his class after break and caught us singing a Rooky song to the tune of the Archies' huge hit, 'Sugar, Sugar'. He told us off for rudeness, and I wanted to say it wasn't rude, it was ... I don't know, affection? Hero worship? Love? We cultivated the use of the word 'Splendid', his highest praise, using it in all other classes to the amusement of our peers.

There was just one occasion where he was really angry with this class, with David and John and Colin and Dougie and Graham and Pete and Alasdair and Richard and everyone else, and it was nothing to do with English. It was Second Year and we were next door in Room 66, having Geography with a nice old lady, a minister's wife, who had been called in to do cover while our teacher was absent. We were noisy and silly and bored, so she went to fetch Mr Caw. He came in, saw it was us, and looked so sad. Then he shouted at us, telling us that he was utterly disappointed and that if he heard another word out of place he would 'belt every one of you'. I wonder if he would have; I think it might have killed him. But, of course, he didn't have to.

I remember returning to school after Christmas in 1973. I was fifteen, going on sixteen, and there was a sharp divide between those who had been 'out' at New Year and those of us who had remained in the parental home. I fell very firmly into the latter, I suspect larger, group, but there were certainly some who had been to parties and may even have smelled some shandy. They expected to be regarded with awe. Mr Caw asked a few of us what we had done on New Year's Eve, including me. 'I went to bed early, with Mrs Gaskell,' I said, with no intention of humour. Mr Caw thought this hilarious. The rest of the class were nonplussed, there being perhaps three others who knew who she was. One guy – even in the top set – asked me if she was a lunch-lady.

At Christmas again, about thirty years after I left school, I drove to Annan in Dumfriesshire – a town to which one does not go lightly – for his funeral. I had last seen him about three years before he died, and before he moved back to Annan, which was where he was from. I bumped into him on a sunny day in the summer holidays; he was in the school office, giving them an obituary of his wife, who had also worked at the school, teaching Maths; she had been ill for a while, but died suddenly. On that day he called me 'Cameron' for the first time to my face, and I, at fifty, number two in the school, very shyly called him Jim. I walked with him into the Quadrangle and offered him tea; he declined but started to tell me about his wife's death, then quite suddenly was in tears, and embarrassed, fled. I wrote to him, but never heard back and I never saw him again.

Most of us have a favourite teacher and teachers themselves always have one: a quirk of timetabling places us in a classroom with someone who can, by slow increments, inspire us and mould us, give us confidence and help us know things.

I went to Rooky's funeral because he had changed my life: I taught English because he taught me. He wrote to me when I started teaching, and again when I went to Heriot's as Head of English. He was a wise and clever and modest man; I doubt he would have really believed his importance in my life. I don't suppose there is a greater tribute to a man's career than to imitate it. I remember his gentle voice teaching us as the rain pattered off the cupola in Room 65, and I can still recite Keats' 'On First Looking into Chapman's Homer', which I learnt there when I was twelve.

Thank you, Rooky.

A Last Lunch with Robert

The period leading up to my retirement was absolutely beautiful. People were very kind. I only cried once.

On a December's morning, with ten days to do till the end of my career, Robert Dickson, by now the Head of the Senior School, phoned to say he had to see me; he must come to my office immediately. He arrived looking very serious, and began to talk about a disciplinary thing in S3 that I already knew about.

'I know about that,' I said, perplexed. 'And don't we have our regular meeting scheduled for 9.00?' This was 8.52.

'Yes, yes,' he said, 'but it's just really important.'

A knock at the door. A First Year boy.

'Sorry, I'm busy,' I said.

'Eh . . . there are some important people out here who want to see you,' the child said, smiling away. And Robert was smiling away too.

The office was strangely quiet as the boy led me outside into the Quadrangle, where the Pipe Band had assembled and immediately began to play Christmas carols. The snow was falling; I stood alone, watched by a crowd of staff and pupils, with more kids watching from the brightly lit windows of the Old Building. They played; the Pipe Major gave me a beautiful gift to recognise my support of the Pipe Band, and I cried.

Back inside, Christy, my PA and life-support machine, apologised: 'I thought it would be nice if I filmed it, but really, I should have stood beside you.'

I have the film. I have not watched it all through yet.

My retirement was like Frank Sinatra's final tour. Every day something nice would happen: a child, now a grown woman, would appear to thank me for dealing with her mother twenty years before; someone gave me a tree; there was lots of booze; a medal; a clock; an antique picture of George Heriot given to me by a boy whose dad I had taught at Stewart's Melville; the Junior School sang the 'Twelve Days of Christmas', the staff's bit being a lusty 'FIVE GOLD RINGS!' I felt waves of affection towards me which, in truth, I had not really felt since I taught in a classroom. So I feared the day it would stop.

On that last day, I attended the usual carol service and returned to my bare office. I knew the school would feel desolate immediately, so I was taking Robert out for lunch.

I have been blessed in my life with great people to work with, all the way from the English department at Stewart's to the School Management Team which was in place at Heriot's when I left. I have been lucky with my bosses – particularly Keith Pearson who was my first Head at Heriot's – and lucky with colleagues and lucky with all the people who helped me. But most of all I was lucky with Robert, who was the first person I appointed to a job when I became the Head of English at Heriot's; who then became the Head of Department himself, then an Assistant Head, then Head of Senior School. He was there all through, this Glasgow policeman's son, a fair and just family man, honest, straight down the line, serious, hardworking, organised, respected. In other words, just about as different to me as it would be possible to be. But we were, for a while, the yin and yang which was part of the school's success. And we had 300k laughs along the way.

So Robert and I had lunch, a good lunch, we had a bottle of white Rioja and we were maybe just a bit subdued. Tired, of course, but there was something else. We then walked along past the Castle towards the West End and there we parted ways, him to get his bus to South Queensferry, me to go home and retire. I knew it would be some time till I saw Robert again, him and all the others, now home to their families for Christmas. Who, I thought, would I ever see?

It was dark and a bit foggy, six days before Christmas, and as I walked along Princes Street I thought, now it is all over. Now there are no more speeches to give or gifts to accept or letters to write or thank yous to say. No more Junior School kids running up to say hello. No more leavers' balls. Just me and Kevin and the house and garden. Books. Films. Food. Drink. Travel. Friends. I waited for a low black cloud to descend on my brain, foggy itself with wine.

And then I thought, naaah, forget that, I'll go and have a coffee in Harvey Nichols. I never buy anything there, but I've got the app, so the coffee is free. I did that, then got on a 26 to Joppa, and retirement's been fine, thanks.

Thank you, Robert and all the other staff who were my friends, and covered for me.

Chips

So I imagine myself lying on my deathbed and thinking about my life. If this was to happen tomorrow, I hope I would not be complaining, but thinking about how lucky I have been. Lucky with my childhood, lucky with my education, lucky with my partner, lucky with my health, lucky with my friends, and really, really lucky with my job. I think my one regret might be that I did not have children of my own. Of course I saved on all that worry and the vomit on the floor and the suspicious powder and the unsuitable friends, and I saved a busload of money, but there is maybe something of a void there which may have made me rather selfish; no matter how much I might have loved my non-existent grandchildren, I cannot think I would ever have wanted to look after them for a day or two a week while my child, their parent, pursued their career in what? The law? Drag artistry? Prison?

The strangest thing about my life – to date, I mean, something stranger could happen tomorrow – are my friends.

Friends have always been really important to me. After I had come out – another story, another book – my discomfited mother, never easy anyway, got at me one day. I was, she said, too dependent on my friends – they would all marry, and have children and forget me. I would be lonely and on my own. She was not herself an advert for family life, in truth, though she mellowed in later years, and I loved her anyway, but it did worry me. In the event, she was wrong – I have many, many friends as I gaze into the middle-distance of old age and I think, if my brain or my body ever lets go, some of them would still come to see me.

Here, at sixty-four, I spend about half my social time with former pupils, and I have had people I have taught as pals for a very long time now, almost from the start of my career. It took me ages to realise how extremely odd this was.

It happened because, on a summer day in 1981, at the end of my first year of teaching, I was visiting Elizabeth Dorward, my colleague and mentor and friend, in her big, elegant house in Murrayfield. We were sitting in her kitchen, which was about the size of my flat, and I was telling her stories and making her laugh. The doorbell rang and she reappeared with three young men. It turned out they were boys whom she had taught years before, now come home from university for the summer, and just dropping by to see her. So they stayed and ate her biscuits with me and we all laughed a great deal more. And that was that – I just assumed that when you had taught people they might come and see you. And so it was for me forever. Every year, after they left school, I would see some students, mostly – not always – who had gone on to uni. They would write to me and I would write back. They would come and see me. I would buy them cakes. Some of them are in their fifties now.

I didn't realise how fully weird this was until an afternoon, twelve years after that lovely summer's day at Elizabeth's house, when I was at a Heads of Department meeting at Heriot's. One of the janitors came in and said that someone had appeared to see me, and indeed, it was a cheerful, clever boy whom I had taught the previous year and who was home from Glasgow University for Christmas; he had, somehow or other, convinced the janitor that his visit was urgent. We agreed a time to meet and he went away. I happened to be sitting next to another of this young man's former teachers, and I knew they liked each other.

At the end of the meeting I said, 'That was Dicky Chancer in to see me.'

My colleague, a clever, serious, intense man said, 'Oh, yes. What did he want?'

'He was just in to see me.'

He stopped and looked at me. 'But what did he want?'

'Just to say hello, I suppose.'

He laughed. 'I don't think that's ever happened to me.'

By this time, it had happened to me lots, but I began to realise it was me who was unusual.

Of course, it's all taboo now. Teachers are advised not to be on Facebook, lest it means some deranged pupil can see pictures of your puppies or, worse, you can see photos of their birthday party. It's all so sad.

Stewart's Melville was an all-boys school. These were not times when young gay men adopted or had their own children. I think I knew, even at twenty-five, I would never likely have children of my own. I was unabashedly sentimental about schools. I pictured myself lying on my deathbed, like Mr Chips. In that heart-jangling novel, the old schoolteacher, having been widowed decades before and then, like myself, rather unexpectedly and late in his career become the Headmaster of the school he loves, is on his deathbed. He overhears his colleagues talking about him:

' "I thought I heard you – one of you – saying it was a pity – umph – a pity I never had – any children ... eh? ... But I have, you know ... I have ..."

' "Yes – umph – I have," he added, with quavering merriment. "Thousands of 'em ... thousands of 'em ... and all boys ..." '

Well, who knows – or cares – what Education Scotland or the GTCS would have to say, but when I taught at Stewart's Melville, I thought that might be me. I would die without real family, but content to be remembered well by thousands of my pupils.

Then I went to Heriot's, which is mixed, and I realised that lying on my deathbed saying 'I had thousands of children, all boys and girls ...' prior to succumbing wouldn't be quite as effective. And by 2021, of course, I knew I would have to say 'I had thousands of children, all boys and girls and those who prefer not to be defined by gender', which might be a bit pernickety for those straining to hear my last utterance. In fact, I hope that like Pitt the Younger, I die asking for one of the excellent pies from Jacky's shop up the road.

But still, boys and girls and those of you who prefer not to be defined by gender, even if it's not very professional, I have loved you and I thank you for your friendship, your kindness, your presents and your presence, your patience and your indulgence as, increasingly, I just talk and talk and talk. Thank you all.

Thank you, Tom

Thank you, Alex

Thank you, Jennifer

Thank you, Malc

Thank you, Euan

Thank you, Faye

Thank you, Nick

Thank you, Beccy

Thank you, Charlie and Francis and Archie

Thank you, Dave and Jamie, for the ukulele and the lessons

Thank you, David and Josh and Alfie.

Thank you, David and Alan and Kevin

Thank you, Jeremy and Gav and Steven and Sir Martin and John and Calum and Richard and Dan the Man, MSP

Thank you, Gabriel and Thomas

Thank you, Tim

Thank you, Calum

Thank you, Kymm (and Kassy) and Linz

Thank you, Scott

Thank you, Rob

Thank you, Emun and Julia

Thank you, Kelsey

Thank you, Ben and OJ and Robert and James and Sandy

Thank you, Paul and Paul and Martin and Lynne (I told you), and Laura and Sarah and Jane and Ruth

Thank you, Donald and Sally and Sandy and Tara Jane and Andy (don't be so hard on yourself) and Laura and Sam RW and Ian and

Thank You

Roisin and Ingrid and Joni and Abigail and Alasdair and Sara and Fiona and Paul(ie) and Joanne (see you Tuesday) and Nick and Jordan and Jenna and Ben and Neil and David and Juliet and Nick and John and Stan and Gavin and Gavin and Nick and George and Rory and Lucy and Noah and Paul and Aoife and Richard and Rahul and Roshini and Rachel and Richard and Richard and Chris and Vanessa and Hannah-Louise (and your mum and your gran) and young David (and your mum and dad) and Andy and Katie and Kate and Natalie and Brian and Merrick and MSP and PMW and Mark and Roger and Stuart and Calum and Ben and Sam Z and Chris and Hannah and Georgie and Diana and Pandy the poet and Professor Watty and Andrew (I genuinely thought you would be Prime Minister).

Thank you all for being my friends. And for buying this book because your name's in it.

Acknowledgements

Thanks to everyone who is mentioned in this book. Some names are real, some are changed and some are ridiculous.

I would like to thank my agent, Judy Moir, for her energy and optimism, and everyone at Birlinn for taking me on.

Thank you to Grant Munro and Rebecca Lassen for agreeing to let me use their wonderful poems. Thanks also to Patsy Seddon for allowing me to use the lyrics of Davy Steele's 'Just One More Chorus'.

Thank you to Stewart Adams and Lesley Franklin; so often my association with the Junior School was a great solace!

Thank you to everyone who read parts of this and encouraged me, but particular thanks to Iain Scott, who has been unfailingly positive about everything I do for a long time now. It is much appreciated.